ADVANCED ENGINE
PERFORMANCE DIAGNOSIS

A Worktext

James D. Halderman

Sinclair Community College

Prentice Hall
Upper Saddle River, New Jersey   Columbus, Ohio

© 1998 by Prentice-Hall, Inc.
Simon & Schuster/A Viacom Company
Upper Saddle River, New Jersey 07458

Printed in the United States of America

10 9 8 7 6 5 4 3 2

ISBN: 0-13-576570-6

TL
210
.H287
1998
WORTEXT

PREFACE

This worktext was developed to help students (and instructors) learn about automotive engine performance diagnosis. It includes real-life practical worksheets that can be used in a classroom, demonstration, or laboratory setting. Most worksheets include specifications, procedures, and anticipated results. This worktext is designed to be used along with the ADVANCED ENGINE PERFORMANCE DIAGNOSIS textbook.

Also included in this worktext are typical handouts for use by the students. This saves time spent in duplicating hundreds of copies of various handout materials. **With this worktext, all materials are in one easy-to-find-and-use location.**

The material in this worktext has been extensively field tested for several years. This worktext has also been used during seminars at national automotive teacher conferences with excellent comments and reviews.

James D. Halderman

TABLE OF CONTENTS

UNIT 7   ENGINE FUELS AND DRIVEABILITY DIAGNOSIS

UNIT 8   COMPUTER SENSOR TESTING

UNIT 13   ENGINE CONDITION DIAGNOSIS

UNIT 14   SYMPTOM-BASED DIAGNOSIS

APPENDIX

UNIT 1

DIAGNOSTIC PROCESS CHECKS

ENGINE PERFORMANCE DIAGNOSIS WORKSHEET
(To Be Filled Out By the Vehicle Owner)

Name: _____ Mileage: _____ Date: _____

Make: _____ Model: _____ Year: _____ Engine: _____

(PLEASE CIRCLE ALL THAT APPLY IN ALL CATEGORIES)	
Describe Problem:	
When Did the Problem First Occur?	• Just Started • Last Week • Last Month • Other _____
List Previous Repairs in the Last 6 Months:	
Starting Problems	• Will Not Crank • Cranks, But Will Not Start • Starts, But Takes A Long Time
Engine Quits or Stalls	• Right After Starting • When Put Into Gear • During Steady Speed Driving • Right After Vehicle Comes To a Stop •While Idling • During Acceleration • When Parking
Poor Idling Conditions	• Is Too Slow At All Times • Is Too Fast •Intermittently Too Fast or Too Slow • Is Rough or Uneven • Fluctuates Up and Down
Poor Running Conditions	• Runs Rough • Lacks Power • Bucks and Jerks • Poor Fuel Economy • Hesitates or Stumbles On Acceleration • Backfires • Misfires or Cuts Out • Engine Knocks, Pings, Rattles • Surges • Dieseling or Run-On
Auto. Transmission Problems	• Improper Shifting (early/late) • Changes Gear Incorrectly • Vehicle Does Not Move When In Gear • Jerks or Bucks
Usually Occurs	• Morning • Afternoon • Anytime
Engine Temperature	• Cold • Warm • Hot
Driving Conditions During Occurrence	• Short-Less Than 2 Miles • 2-10 Miles • Long-More Than 10 Miles • Stop and Go • While Turning • While Braking • At Gear Engagement • With A/C Operating • With Headlights On • During Acceleration • During Deceleration • Mostly Downhill • Mostly Uphill • Mostly Level • Mostly Curvy • Rough Road
Driving Habits	• Mostly City Driving • Highway • Park Vehicle Inside • Park Vehicle Outside **Drive Per Day:** • Less Than 10 Miles • 10-50 • More Than 50
Gasoline Used	**Fuel Octane:** • 87 • 89 • 91 • More Than 91 **Brand:** _____
Temperature When Problem Occurs	• 32-55° F • Below Freezing (32° F) • Above 55° F
Check Engine Light/ Dash Warning Light	• Light on Sometimes • Light on Always • Light Never On
Smells	• "Hot" • Gasoline • Oil Burning • Electrical
Noises	• Rattle • Knock • Squeak • Other

NAME_____

MAKE_____ MODEL_____ YR_____

EVIDENCE OF PREVIOUS REPAIRS WORKSHEET

_____ 1. Check for a recent oil change.

    A. The incorrect viscosity of oil could have been installed.
    B. The incorrect oil filter could have been installed.

_____ 2. Check for recent body work.

    A. Ground wires could be left disconnected, loose or attached to a painted (insulated) surface.
    B. Windshield replacement could cause water leaks to get into computers or wiring.
    C. Electrical connectors could be disconnected.
    D. Wiring could have been spliced or repaired - look for improper repair procedure that could lead to corrosion or high electrical resistance.

_____ 3. Check for recent clutch or transmission repairs.

    A. Collapsed mounts can cause vibration.
    B. A dislocated cradle can cause pulling to one side.
    C. Many ground wires may have been left unattached.

_____ 4. Recent filter changes or PCV replacement.

The probability of the incorrect part number being installed can cause driveability problems.

OK _____ NOT OK _____

DATE_____

_____
INSTRUCTOR'S OK

NAME_____

MAKE_____ MODEL_____ YR_____

PAPER TEST WORKSHEET

_____ 1. The engine should be at normal operating temperature (the upper radiator hot and pressurized).

_____ 2. Check the exhaust system for leaks (test results may not be valid if the exhaust system is not okay).

_____ 3. Start the engine and allow it to idle. A sound running engine should produce even and steady exhaust "puffs" at the tailpipe.

_____ 4. Hold a piece of paper (even a dollar bill works) or a 3" x 5" card within 1 inch (2.5 cm) of the tailpipe with the engine running at idle. The paper should blow out evenly without "puffing".

    A. If the paper is drawn toward the tailpipe at times, the valves in one or more cylinders could be burned. Other possible problems if the paper is sucked toward the tailpipe include:
        1) the engine could be misfiring due to a lean condition that could occur normally when the engine is cold.
        2) a hole in the exhaust system. If exhaust escapes through a hole in the exhaust system, air could be drawn from the tailpipe to the hole in the exhaust between the exhaust "puffs," causing the paper to be drawn toward the tailpipe.

    B. If the paper is unevenly pulsing outward, an engine misfire is a possibility. The usual cause of this is an ignition or an engine mechanical problem such as a worn camshaft or broken rocker arm.

_____ 5. Describe the results _____

_____

OK____   NOT OK____

DATE_____

_____
INSTRUCTOR'S OK

NAME_____

MAKE_____ MODEL_____ YR_____

DIPSTICK TEST WORKSHEET

_____ 1. Check for proper oil level on dipstick:

      _____ oil level overfilled

      _____ oil level correct

      _____ oil level low

_____ 2. Ignite the oil on the dipstick:

      _____ does not burn

      _____ does burn

      NOTE: If the oil on the dipstick burns, there is gasoline in the oil. This will cause the engine to run rich by drawing the fuel through the PCV system. Gasoline in the oil can also damage the engine due to the diluted oil not properly lubricating the engine.

_____ 3. Drip oil onto the hot exhaust manifold:

      _____ does not bubble

      _____ does bubble

      NOTE: If the oil bubbles on the exhaust manifold, coolant (water) is in the oil.

_____ 4. Rub the oil from the dipstick between your fingers:

      _____ does not feel gritty

      _____ does feel gritty

DATE_____

INSTRUCTOR'S OK
_____

NAME_____

MAKE_____ MODEL_____ YR____

FLUIDS AND FILTERS INSPECTION WORKSHEET

_____ 1. Check the condition of the air filter.

_____ 2. Check the engine oil (do not overfill).

_____ 3. Check the condition of the crankcase vent filter.

_____ 4. Check the brake fluid level (should be 1/4" from the top).

_____ 5. Check all radiator and heater hoses (check for cracks, swollen, brittle, or leaking hose).

_____ 6. Check the battery "eye" water level (if possible).

_____ 7. Clean the battery and tighten all connections.

_____ 8. Check the power steering fluid (use power steering fluid only unless otherwise specified).

_____ 9. Check the radiator coolant level (check when cold only!). The coolant should be within 3" of the top of the filler neck. (The reserve tank should be filled to the indicated mark.)

_____ 10. Check the automatic transmission fluid with the engine running at idle, the vehicle on level ground, the transmission in neutral (or park) and the transmission hot. If the level of the fluid is not between "add" and "full", correct the fluid level as required.

   NOTE: The add mark means - add 1 pint (1/2 quart).

DATE_____

_____
INSTRUCTOR'S OK

NAME_____

MAKE_____ MODEL_____ YR_____

ACCESSORY DRIVE BELT INSPECTION WORKSHEET

Proper operation of the alternator and the charging system as well as the water (coolant) pump and other cooling systems depend on the accessory drive belt(s).

Serpentine (poly-V) belt:

1. Check for cracks - replace if more than 3 cracks in any one rib in 3 inches.

2. Check for proper tension - check the tensioner notch location for proper tension position.
   OK ____ NOT OK ____

V-belts:

1. Check belt tension:

   A. usual specifications: 70 to 100 lbs. of tension using a belt tension gauge.
   B. maximum of ½ in. deflection.

   OK ____ NOT OK ____

2. Check the belt for flaying, cracks and glazing.

   OK ____ NOT OK ____

DATE _____

_____   NAME_____

INSTRUCTOR'S OK

MAKE_____ MODEL_____ YR____

FUEL PRESSURE TEST WORKSHEET

Many engine performance problems are caused by low fuel pressure. Low fuel pressure on a fuel-injected vehicle can be caused by a weak electric fuel pump or a defective fuel pressure regulator. Excessively high fuel pressure can be caused by a crimped fuel meter line or a defective fuel pressure regulator.

_____ 1. Disconnect the electric fuel pump fuse (if equipped) or the wiring to the fuel pump and start the engine. Allow it to run until the engine stops, then crank the engine for 15 seconds to deplete any remaining fuel pressure.

_____ 2. Locate the fuel pressure service port (Schrader valve) and connect a fuel pressure gauge to the service port.

   NOTE: Most General Motors throttle body injection systems do <u>not</u> have a Schrader valve to test for fuel pressure. A special fuel pressure gauge is required that connects between the TBI unit and the fuel line going to the TBI unit.

_____ 3. Reconnect the fuel pump fuse or the wiring for the electric fuel pump and start the engine. Observe the fuel pressure.

   Operating fuel pressure = _____

_____ 4. Determine the correct fuel pressure by consulting the service manual or the computer reference material.

   Specified fuel pressure = _____

OK _____ **NOT OK** _____

DATE_____

_____

INSTRUCTOR'S OK

NAME_____

MAKE_____ MODEL_____ YR_____

AIR INTAKE INSPECTION WORKSHEET

Every engine takes in a large quantity of air during its operation. If the airstream leading to the engine is restricted or otherwise defective, the engine will not perform correctly.

_____ 1. Locate and remove the air filter.

      A. Did it fit snugly in the housing? **YES ___ NO ___**

      B. Is the filter wet or deformed?   **YES ___ NO ___**

_____ 2. Inspect the filter for restriction or breaks.

      OK _____   NOT OK _____

_____ 3. Is a new air filter required? **YES ___ NO ___**

_____ 4. Inspect the air duct work from the filter to the outside air source.

      A. Is the passageway open and clean? **YES ___ NO ___**

      B. Is the duct work okay and free from tears or holes? **YES ___ NO ___**

_____ 5. Inspect the air duct work from the filter to the engine inlet.

      A. Is the duct work okay and free from tears or holes? **YES ___ NO ___**

DATE_____

UNIT 2

DIAGNOSTIC TROUBLE CODE RETRIEVAL

_____   NAME_____

INSTRUCTOR'S OK

MAKE_____ MODEL_____ YR_____

CODE RETRIEVAL AND CLEARING WORKSHEET

Retrieving diagnostic trouble codes (DTCs) is an important step that all service technicians should be able to perform as part of a comprehensive diagnostic troubleshooting procedure.

_____ 1. Start and operate the engine until normal operating temperature is achieved.

_____ 2. Disconnect a sensor that is likely to set a diagnostic trouble code such as: the throttle position (TP), mass air flow (MAF) or engine coolant temperature (ECT).

      Unit disconnected = _____

_____ 3. Turn off the ignition and then turn the ignition back on (engine off). Retrieve the stored diagnostic trouble code using the proper procedure.

      Did the code set? Yes _____ What code set? _____

      Did the code set? No _____ Try another sensor until a code is set.

      Description of code fault _____

_____ 4. Clear the diagnostic trouble code by:

      A. using a scan tool
      B. disconnecting the computer fuse or fusible link
      C. disconnecting the battery

      Which method was used? _____

_____ 5. Verify that the DTC has been cleared by retrieving stored diagnostic trouble codes.

_____ 6. What code represents that everything is OK? _____

DATE_____

_____
INSTRUCTOR'S OK

NAME_____

MAKE_____ MODEL_____ YR_____

SET OPPOSITE CODE WORKSHEET

If a diagnostic trouble code is set, a commonly used method of diagnosis is to attempt to set the opposite code after clearing the original code. For example, if a throttle position (TP) code is set, clear the DTC and attempt to set a DTC for the opposite condition.

- If a signal high DTC is set, clear the code and turn the ignition switch on (engine off), unplug the sensor and a signal low DTC should be set.

- If a signal low DTC is set, unplug the sensor connector and using a jumper wire, connect the 5-volt reference to the signal terminal in the connector (not at the sensor). Turn the ignition switch on (engine off) and the opposite DTC should set.

_____ 1. Set a DTC for TP or MAP sensor.

      A. Which sensor was used? _____
      B. What code set? _____
      C. Meaning of code set? _____

_____ 2. Clear the DTC.

_____ 3. Disconnect the sensor wiring and use a jumper wire to set the opposite code.

      A. What code was set? _____
      B. **OK** _____ **NOT OK** _____

Results:

If the opposite code <u>does</u> set, the cause of the original DTC is the result of a fault in the sensor (component) itself.

If the opposite DTC <u>does not</u> set, the problem is likely due to a wiring fault.

NOTE: Always consult a factory service manual for the factors that must be met for a DTC to be set. Be sure that all factors are present when attempting to set the opposite code.

DATE _____

_____
INSTRUCTOR'S OK

NAME_____

MAKE_____ MODEL_____ YR_____

RETRIEVING GENERAL MOTORS DIAGNOSTIC TROUBLE CODES WORKSHEET

Flash codes can be retrieved from most General Motors vehicles from 1981 through 1995. (Some 1993, 1994 and 1995 models cannot display flash codes - to retrieve DTC from these vehicles, a scan tool is **required**.)

_____ 1. Locate the data link connector (DLC) formerly called the ALCL or ALDC.

      A. usually located under the dash near the steering column.
      B. Fieros DLC is located between the seats. The lighter panel has to be removed to gain access.
      C. Corvette DLC is located under the ash tray in the center console.

_____ 2. Turn the ignition switch to on (engine off). "Check engine" light should be on. If it is not on, stop and consult a service manual for the procedure to follow including checking the bulb.

_____ 3. Using the appropriate tool, connect terminals "A" and "B". The amber "check engine" light should flash once, then pause, then flash twice. (This is a code 12 which indicates that the computer is capable of self diagnosis.

_____ 4. Was a code 12 displayed? Yes ___ No ___

_____ 5. List all other DTCs displayed:

    _____ _____ _____ _____ _____

_____ 6. Connect a TECH 1 or TECH 2 scan tool (if available) and retrieve the DTCs. List all codes displayed on the scan tool:

    _____ _____ _____ _____ _____

_____ 7. Connect a generic scan tool (if available) and retrieve the DTCs. List all codes displayed on the scan tool:

    _____ _____ _____ _____ _____

_____ 8. Did the scan tool(s) display the same DTC as the flash code method? Yes ___ No ___

DATE_____

INSTRUCTOR'S OK

NAME_____

MAKE_____ MODEL_____ YR____

RETRIEVING FORD DIAGNOSTIC TROUBLE CODES WORKSHEET

_____ 1. Perform "key on, engine off, self test" using a voltmeter or test light. List all retrieved DTCs:

_____ _____ _____ _____ _____

_____ 2. Perform an "engine running self test" using a voltmeter or test light. List all retrieved DTCs:

_____ _____ _____ _____ _____

_____ 3. Perform a complete diagnosis using a STAR tester. List all retrieved DTCs:

_____ _____ _____ _____ _____

_____ 4. Retrieve the DTCs using a generic scan tool. List all retrieved DTCs:

_____ _____ _____ _____ _____

_____ 5. Did this scan tool(s) display the same DTC as was retrieved using the flash codes method?   Yes ___ No ___

DATE_____

_____

INSTRUCTOR'S OK

NAME_____

MAKE_____ MODEL_____ YR_____

RETRIEVING CHRYSLER DIAGNOSTIC TROUBLE CODES WORKSHEET

Trouble code information is displayed only for major problems. The computer checks a number of functions when the engine starts and monitors other functions while the engine is running. Codes of intermittent faults are stored in memory for approximately 50 start-ups. If the fault does not reoccur within the fifty start-ups, the computer is programmed to erase the code from memory. If the fault reoccurs, the fault code is again retained in memory (but retained for one hundred engine starts if the same code is set again).

To put the computer into the self-diagnostic mode, the ignition switch must be turned on and off twice within a 5-second period. The computer will flash a series of fault codes in a manner similar to the GM system. Early models of Chrysler products used a light-emitting diode (LED) located on the side of the logic module, which was located behind the kick panel and behind a plastic plug. Newer Chrysler products flash the "power loss", "power limited" or "check engine" lamp on the dash.

See OBD II diagnostic trouble codes for 1996 or newer vehicles. Refer to service information for a description of Chrysler-specific alphanumeric DTCs.

_____ 1. Check for any trouble codes by cycling the ignition key on, off, on, off, then on again in 5 seconds. List the stored DTCs and their meanings:

_____ = _____ ; _____ = _____ ; _____ = _____ ;

_____ = _____ ; _____ = _____ ; _____ = _____ .

_____ 2. Retrieve the DTCs using a generic scan tool (Snap-on, Monitor 4000, or etc.)

_____   _____   _____   _____   _____

_____ 3. Check the vehicle using a DRB II or DRB III Chrysler specific scan tool (if available). List the stored DTCs.

_____   _____   _____   _____   _____

_____ 4. Did this scan tool(s) display the same DTC as was retrieved using the flash codes method?   Yes ___   No ___

DATE_____

_____
INSTRUCTOR'S OK

NAME_____

MAKE_____ MODEL_____ YR_____

RETRIEVING HONDA DIAGNOSTIC TROUBLE CODES

The electronic control module (ECM) is found in different locations depending on exact model and year. Most computers are located under the driver's or passenger's seat or under the passenger's floor panel. The diagnostic trouble codes are read by simply turning the ignition on (engine off) and counting the flashes of the LED. Early models used LEDs that could be viewed without having to remove a cover.

The DLC for 1991 and newer Honda models requires that a jumper wire be used to connect it; then the amber MIL on the dash labeled "check engine" must be watched for trouble codes.

_____ 1. Retrieve the stored flash codes and record their meanings:

_____ = _____ ; _____ = _____ ; _____ = _____ ;

_____ = _____ ; _____ = _____ ; _____ = _____ .

_____ 2. Retrieve the DTCs using a scan tool.

(Specify which scan tool was used = _____).

_____ _____ _____ _____ _____

_____ 3. Did this scan tool(s) display the same DTC as was retrieved using the flash codes method?   Yes ___   No ___

DATE_____

NAME_____

MAKE_____ MODEL_____ YR_____

RETRIEVING TOYOTA DIAGNOSTIC TROUBLE CODES

Toyota vehicles use the "check engine" MIL to display diagnostic trouble codes. See OBD II diagnostic trouble codes for 1996 or newer vehicles. Refer to service information for a description of Toyota-specific alphanumeric DTCs.

_____ 1. Retrieve the stored flash codes and record their meanings:

_____ = _____ ; _____ = _____ ; _____ = _____ ;

_____ = _____ ; _____ = _____ ; _____ = _____ .

_____ 2. Retrieve the DTCs using a scan tool.

(Specify which scan tool was used = _____ .)

_____ _____ _____ _____ _____

_____ 3. Did this scan tool(s) display the same DTC as was retrieved using the flash codes method?   Yes ___   No ___

SERVICE CONNECTOR

CHECK CONNECTOR

TE1

E1

JUMPER WIRE

DATE_____

NAME_____

MAKE_____ MODEL_____ YR_____

RETRIEVING OBD II VEHICLE DIAGNOSTIC TROUBLE CODES

A scan tool is required to retrieve diagnostic trouble codes from an OBD II vehicle. Every OBD II scan tool will be able to read all generic **Society of Automotive Engineers (SAE)** DTCs from any vehicle.

_____ 1. Retrieve the DTCs using a scan tool.

(Specify which scan tool was used = _____.)

_____   _____   _____   _____   _____

_____ 2. If no DTCs are displayed, set a DTC by disconnecting a sensor such as the throttle position (TP) sensor and then starting and running the engine.

_____ 3. Did the scan tool display both a generic OBD II (Poxxx) code <u>and</u> a manufacturer's specific DTC (P1xxx) code?

Yes _____   No _____

_____ 4. Clear the stored DTCs using the scan tool.

DATE_____

UNIT 3

TECHNICAL SERVICE BULLETINS (TSBs) AND SCAN TOOL DATA

NAME_____

MAKE_____ MODEL_____ YR_____

MITCHELL-ON-DEMAND WORKSHEET

_____ 1. Select the proper make, model, and year CD-ROM disk.

_____ 2. List 4 technical service bulletins that may affect your vehicle:

      A. _____

      B. _____

      C. _____

      D. _____

_____ 3. Determine the following information about your vehicle:

      spark plug number: _____

      spark plug gap: _____

      ignition timing specification (if possible): _____

      firing order: _____

      oil filter number: _____

_____ 4. Exit the program.

DATE_____

_____
INSTRUCTOR'S OK

NAME_____

MAKE_____ MODEL_____ YR_____

ALLDATA WORKSHEET

_____ 1. Select the proper make, model, and year CD-ROM disk.

_____ 2. List 4 technical service bulletins that may affect your vehicle:

     A. _____

     B. _____

     C. _____

     D. _____

_____ 3. Determine the following information about your vehicle:

     spark plug number: _____

     spark plug gap: _____

     firing order: _____

     oil filter number: _____

_____ 4. Return to the main menu.

DATE_____

NAME_____

MAKE_____ MODEL_____ YR_____

MOPAR DIAGNOSTIC SYSTEM (MDS) WORKSHEET

_____ 1. Select the make, model, and year or VIN number for the vehicle being checked.

_____ 2. List 4 technical service bulletins that may affect your vehicle:

      A. _____

      B. _____

      C. _____

      D. _____

_____ 3. Determine the following information about your vehicle and record the following information:

      spark plug number: _____

      spark plug gap: _____

      firing order: _____

      oil filter number: _____

_____ 4. Return to the main menu.

DATE_____

_____
INSTRUCTOR'S OK

NAME_____

MAKE_____ MODEL_____ YR_____

GENERAL MOTORS TECHLINE SYSTEM WORKSHEET
(T-65, etc.)

_____ 1. Select a General Motors vehicle that is covered by the Techline equipment available.

_____ 2. List 4 technical service bulletins that may affect the vehicle:

      A. _____

      B. _____

      C. _____

      D. _____

_____ 3. Determine the following information about the vehicle and record the following information:

      spark plug number: _____

      spark plug gap: _____

      main bearing oil clearance: _____

      firing order: _____

      oil filter number: _____

_____ 4. Return to the main menu.

DATE_____

_____   NAME_____
INSTRUCTOR'S OK

MAKE_____ MODEL_____ YR_____

"TECH I" DATA RETRIEVAL WORKSHEET

(Not all of this data will be available on all vehicles or scan tools - if not available, put NA.)

1. Trouble codes: _____ PROM ID:_____

2. Engine coolant temperature (ECT): cold _____ warm _____

3. Intake air temperature (IAT):   cold _____ warm _____

4. Upstream O2S1:   lowest voltage observed _____ highest voltage observed _____

5. Upstream O2S2:   lowest voltage observed _____ highest voltage observed _____

6. Downstream O2S: lowest voltage observed _____ highest voltage observed _____

7. O_2 cross counts: @ idle____ @ 2,000 RPM____

8. Injector pulse width: @ idle (park)_____ @ idle (drive)_____

   @ 2,000 RPM (park)_____ @ 3,000 RPM (park)_____

9. Spark advance: @ idle (park)_____ @ idle (drive)_____

   @ 2,000 RPM (park)_____ @ 3,000 RPM (park)_____

10. Short term fuel trim (integrator): @ idle (park)_____

   @ idle (drive)_____ @ 2,000 RPM (park)_____

11. Long term fuel trim (block learn): @ idle (park)_____ @ idle (drive)_____

12. P/N switch: OK_____ NOT OK_____

13. P/S switch: OK_____ NOT OK_____

14. MAP: @ idle (park)_____ @ idle (drive)_____

15. MAF (grams/sec): @ idle (park)_____ @ idle (drive)_____

   @ 2,000 RPM (park)_____ @ key on (engine off)_____

16. IAC counts: @ idle (park)_____ @ idle (drive)_____

   @ A/C on (drive)_____ @ 2,000 RPM (park)_____

17. Throttle position (TP) sensor: @ idle_____ @ W.O.T. engine off, ignition "on"_____

18. Battery voltage:_____

19. Troubles with the vehicle? (if any)_____

DATE_____

INSTRUCTOR'S OK
_____

NAME_____

MAKE_____ MODEL_____ YR_____

"TECH 2" DATA RETRIEVAL WORKSHEET

(Not all of this data will be available on all vehicles or scan tools - if not available, put NA.)

1. Trouble codes: _____ PROM ID:_____

2. Engine coolant temperature (ECT): cold _____ warm _____

3. Intake air temperature (IAT):   cold _____ warm _____

4. Upstream O2S1:   lowest voltage observed _____ highest voltage observed _____

5. Upstream O2S2:   lowest voltage observed _____ highest voltage observed _____

6. Downstream O2S: lowest voltage observed _____ highest voltage observed _____

7. O_2 cross counts: @ idle____ @ 2,000 RPM____

8. Injector pulse width: @ idle (park)_____ @ idle (drive)_____

    @ 2,000 RPM (park)_____ @ 3,000 RPM (park)_____

9. Spark advance: @ idle (park)_____ @ idle (drive)_____

    @ 2,000 RPM (park)_____ @ 3,000 RPM (park)_____

10. Short term fuel trim (integrator): @ idle (park)_____

    @ idle (drive)_____ @ 2,000 RPM (park)_____

11. Long term fuel trim (block learn): @ idle (park)_____ @ idle (drive)_____

12. P/N switch: OK_____ NOT OK_____

13. P/S switch: OK_____ NOT OK_____

14. MAP: @ idle (park)_____ @ idle (drive)_____

15. MAF (grams/sec): @ idle (park)_____ @ idle (drive)_____

    @ 2,000 RPM (park)_____ @ key on (engine off)_____

16. IAC counts: @ idle (park)_____ @ idle (drive)_____

    @ A/C on (drive)_____ @ 2,000 RPM (park)_____

17. Throttle position (TP) sensor: @ idle_____ @ W.O.T. engine off, ignition "on"_____

18. Battery voltage:_____

19. Troubles with the vehicle? (if any)_____

DATE_____

_____ NAME_____

INSTRUCTOR'S OK

MAKE_____ MODEL_____ YR_____

SNAP-ON SCANNER DATA RETRIEVAL WORKSHEET

(Not all of this data will be available on all vehicles or scan tools - if not available, put NA.)

1. Trouble codes: _____ PROM ID:_____

2. Engine coolant temperature (ECT): cold _____ warm _____

3. Intake air temperature (IAT): cold _____ warm _____

4. Upstream O2S1: lowest voltage observed _____ highest voltage observed _____

5. Upstream O2S2: lowest voltage observed _____ highest voltage observed _____

6. Downstream O2S: lowest voltage observed _____ highest voltage observed _____

7. O_2 cross counts: @ idle____ @ 2,000 RPM____

8. Injector pulse width: @ idle (park)_____ @ idle (drive)_____

   @ 2,000 RPM (park)_____ @ 3,000 RPM (park)_____

9. Spark advance: @ idle (park)_____ @ idle (drive)_____

   @ 2,000 RPM (park)_____ @ 3,000 RPM (park)_____

10. Short term fuel trim (integrator): @ idle (park)_____

    @ idle (drive)_____ @ 2,000 RPM (park)_____

11. Long term fuel trim (block learn): @ idle (park)_____ @ idle (drive)_____

12. P/N switch: OK_____ NOT OK_____

13. P/S switch: OK_____ NOT OK_____

14. MAP: @ idle (park)_____ @ idle (drive)_____

15. MAF (grams/sec): @ idle (park)_____ @ idle (drive)_____

    @ 2,000 RPM (park)_____ @ key on (engine off)_____

16. IAC counts: @ idle (park)_____ @ idle (drive)_____

    @ A/C on (drive)_____ @ 2,000 RPM (park)_____

17. Throttle position (TP) sensor: @ idle_____ @ W.O.T. engine off, ignition "on"_____

18. Battery voltage:_____

19. Troubles with the vehicle? (if any)_____

DATE_____

_____   NAME_____

INSTRUCTOR'S OK

MAKE_____ MODEL_____ YR_____

FORD DATA STREAM RETRIEVAL WORKSHEET

(Not all of this data will be available on all vehicles or scan tools - if not available, put NA.)

1. Trouble codes: _____ PROM ID:_____

2. Engine coolant temperature (ECT): cold _____ warm _____

3. Intake air temperature (IAT): cold _____ warm _____

4. Upstream O2S1: lowest voltage observed _____ highest voltage observed _____

5. Upstream O2S2: lowest voltage observed _____ highest voltage observed _____

6. Downstream O2S: lowest voltage observed _____ highest voltage observed _____

7. O_2 cross counts: @ idle____ @ 2,000 RPM____

8. Injector pulse width: @ idle (park)_____ @ idle (drive)_____

    @ 2,000 RPM (park)_____ @ 3,000 RPM (park)_____

9. Spark advance: @ idle (park)_____ @ idle (drive)_____

    @ 2,000 RPM (park)_____ @ 3,000 RPM (park)_____

10. Short term fuel trim (integrator): @ idle (park)_____

    @ idle (drive)_____ @ 2,000 RPM (park)_____

11. Long term fuel trim (block learn): @ idle (park)_____ @ idle (drive)_____

12. P/N switch: OK_____ NOT OK_____

13. P/S switch: OK_____ NOT OK_____

14. MAP: @ idle (park)_____ @ idle (drive)_____

15. MAF (grams/sec): @ idle (park)_____ @ idle (drive)_____

    @ 2,000 RPM (park)_____ @ key on (engine off)_____

16. IAC counts: @ idle (park)_____ @ idle (drive)_____

    @ A/C on (drive)_____ @ 2,000 RPM (park)_____

17. Throttle position (TP) sensor: @ idle_____ @ W.O.T. engine off, ignition "on"_____

18. Battery voltage:_____

19. Troubles with the vehicle? (if any)_____

DATE_____

_____
INSTRUCTOR'S OK

NAME_____

MAKE_____ MODEL_____ YR_____

"MONITOR 2000" DATA RETRIEVAL WORKSHEET
(Not all of this data will be available on all vehicles or scan tools - if not available, put NA.)

1. Trouble codes: _____ PROM ID:_____

2. Engine coolant temperature (ECT): cold _____ warm _____

3. Intake air temperature (IAT): cold _____ warm _____

4. Upstream O2S1: lowest voltage observed _____ highest voltage observed _____

5. Upstream O2S2: lowest voltage observed _____ highest voltage observed _____

6. Downstream O2S: lowest voltage observed _____ highest voltage observed _____

7. O_2 cross counts: @ idle____ @ 2,000 RPM____

8. Injector pulse width: @ idle (park)_____ @ idle (drive)_____

   @ 2,000 RPM (park)_____ @ 3,000 RPM (park)_____

9. Spark advance: @ idle (park)_____ @ idle (drive)_____

   @ 2,000 RPM (park)_____ @ 3,000 RPM (park)_____

10. Short term fuel trim (integrator): @ idle (park)_____

    @ idle (drive)_____ @ 2,000 RPM (park)_____

11. Long term fuel trim (block learn): @ idle (park)_____ @ idle (drive)_____

12. P/N switch: OK_____ NOT OK_____

13. P/S switch: OK_____ NOT OK_____

14. MAP: @ idle (park)_____ @ idle (drive)_____

15. MAF (grams/sec): @ idle (park)_____ @ idle (drive)_____

    @ 2,000 RPM (park)_____ @ key on (engine off)_____

16. IAC counts: @ idle (park)_____ @ idle (drive)_____

    @ A/C on (drive)_____ @ 2,000 RPM (park)_____

17. Throttle position (TP) sensor: @ idle_____ @ W.O.T. engine off, ignition "on"_____

18. Battery voltage:_____

19. Troubles with the vehicle? (if any)_____

DATE_____

_____   NAME_____

INSTRUCTOR'S OK

MAKE_____ MODEL_____ YR_____

"MONITOR 4000" DATA RETRIEVAL WORKSHEET

(Not all of this data will be available on all vehicles or scan tools - if not available, put NA.)

1. Trouble codes: _____ PROM ID:_____

2. Engine coolant temperature (ECT): cold _____ warm _____

3. Intake air temperature (IAT):   cold _____ warm _____

4. Upstream O2S1:   lowest voltage observed _____ highest voltage observed _____

5. Upstream O2S2:   lowest voltage observed _____ highest voltage observed _____

6. Downstream O2S: lowest voltage observed _____ highest voltage observed _____

7. O_2 cross counts: @ idle____ @ 2,000 RPM____

8. Injector pulse width: @ idle (park)_____ @ idle (drive)_____

   @ 2,000 RPM (park)_____ @ 3,000 RPM (park)_____

9. Spark advance: @ idle (park)_____ @ idle (drive)_____

   @ 2,000 RPM (park)_____ @ 3,000 RPM (park)_____

10. Short term fuel trim (integrator): @ idle (park)_____

    @ idle (drive)_____ @ 2,000 RPM (park)_____

11. Long term fuel trim (block learn): @ idle (park)_____ @ idle (drive)_____

12. P/N switch: OK_____ NOT OK_____

13. P/S switch: OK_____ NOT OK_____

14. MAP: @ idle (park)_____ @ idle (drive)_____

15. MAF (grams/sec): @ idle (park)_____ @ idle (drive)_____

    @ 2,000 RPM (park)_____ @ key on (engine off)_____

16. IAC counts: @ idle (park)_____ @ idle (drive)_____

    @ A/C on (drive)_____ @ 2,000 RPM (park)_____

17. Throttle position (TP) sensor: @ idle_____ @ W.O.T. engine off, ignition "on"_____

18. Battery voltage:_____

19. Troubles with the vehicle? (if any)_____

                                        DATE_____

_____
INSTRUCTOR'S OK

NAME_____

MAKE_____ MODEL_____ YR_____

"BEAR ACE" DATA RETRIEVAL WORKSHEET

(Not all of this data will be available on all vehicles or scan tools - if not available, put NA.)

1. Trouble codes: _____ PROM ID:_____

2. Engine coolant temperature (ECT): cold _____ warm _____

3. Intake air temperature (IAT): cold _____ warm _____

4. Upstream O2S1: lowest voltage observed _____ highest voltage observed _____

5. Upstream O2S2: lowest voltage observed _____ highest voltage observed _____

6. Downstream O2S: lowest voltage observed _____ highest voltage observed _____

7. O_2 cross counts: @ idle____ @ 2,000 RPM____

8. Injector pulse width: @ idle (park)_____ @ idle (drive)_____

    @ 2,000 RPM (park)_____ @ 3,000 RPM (park)_____

9. Spark advance: @ idle (park)_____ @ idle (drive)_____

    @ 2,000 RPM (park)_____ @ 3,000 RPM (park)_____

10. Short term fuel trim (integrator): @ idle (park)_____

    @ idle (drive)_____ @ 2,000 RPM (park)_____

11. Long term fuel trim (block learn): @ idle (park)_____ @ idle (drive)_____

12. P/N switch: OK_____ NOT OK_____

13. P/S switch: OK_____ NOT OK_____

14. MAP: @ idle (park)_____ @ idle (drive)_____

15. MAF (grams/sec): @ idle (park)_____ @ idle (drive)_____

    @ 2,000 RPM (park)_____ @ key on (engine off)_____

16. IAC counts: @ idle (park)_____ @ idle (drive)_____

    @ A/C on (drive)_____ @ 2,000 RPM (park)_____

17. Throttle position (TP) sensor: @ idle_____ @ W.O.T. engine off, ignition "on"_____

18. Battery voltage:_____

19. Troubles with the vehicle? (if any)_____

                                     DATE_____

_____   NAME_____

INSTRUCTOR'S OK

MAKE_____ MODEL_____ YR_____

"MASTER TECH" DATA RETRIEVAL WORKSHEET

(Not all of this data will be available on all vehicles or scan tools - if not available, put NA.)

1. Trouble codes: _____ PROM ID:_____

2. Engine coolant temperature (ECT): cold _____ warm _____

3. Intake air temperature (IAT):   cold _____ warm _____

4. Upstream O2S1:   lowest voltage observed _____ highest voltage observed _____

5. Upstream O2S2:   lowest voltage observed _____ highest voltage observed _____

6. Downstream O2S: lowest voltage observed _____ highest voltage observed _____

7. O_2 cross counts: @ idle____ @ 2,000 RPM____

8. Injector pulse width: @ idle (park)_____ @ idle (drive)_____

    @ 2,000 RPM (park)_____ @ 3,000 RPM (park)_____

9. Spark advance: @ idle (park)_____ @ idle (drive)_____

    @ 2,000 RPM (park)_____ @ 3,000 RPM (park)_____

10. Short term fuel trim (integrator): @ idle (park)_____

    @ idle (drive)_____ @ 2,000 RPM (park)_____

11. Long term fuel trim (block learn): @ idle (park)_____ @ idle (drive)_____

12. P/N switch: OK_____ NOT OK_____

13. P/S switch: OK_____ NOT OK_____

14. MAP: @ idle (park)_____ @ idle (drive)_____

15. MAF (grams/sec): @ idle (park)_____ @ idle (drive)_____

    @ 2,000 RPM (park)_____ @ key on (engine off)_____

16. IAC counts: @ idle (park)_____ @ idle (drive)_____

    @ A/C on (drive)_____ @ 2,000 RPM (park)_____

17. Throttle position (TP) sensor: @ idle_____ @ W.O.T. engine off, ignition "on"_____

18. Battery voltage:_____

19. Troubles with the vehicle? (if any)_____

DATE_____

_____   NAME_____

INSTRUCTOR'S OK

MAKE_____ MODEL_____ YR_____

GENERAL MOTORS TECHLINE DATA RETRIEVAL
WORKSHEET

(Not all of this data will be available on all vehicles or scan tools - if not available, put NA.)

1. Trouble codes: _____ PROM ID:_____

2. Engine coolant temperature (ECT): cold _____ warm _____

3. Intake air temperature (IAT):   cold _____ warm _____

4. Upstream O2S1:   lowest voltage observed _____ highest voltage observed _____

5. Upstream O2S2:   lowest voltage observed _____ highest voltage observed _____

6. Downstream O2S: lowest voltage observed _____ highest voltage observed _____

7. O_2 cross counts: @ idle____ @ 2,000 RPM____

8. Injector pulse width: @ idle (park)_____ @ idle (drive)_____

   @ 2,000 RPM (park)_____ @ 3,000 RPM (park)_____

9. Spark advance: @ idle (park)_____ @ idle (drive)_____

   @ 2,000 RPM (park)_____ @ 3,000 RPM (park)_____

10. Short term fuel trim (integrator): @ idle (park)_____

    @ idle (drive)_____ @ 2,000 RPM (park)_____

11. Long term fuel trim (block learn): @ idle (park)_____ @ idle (drive)_____

12. P/N switch: OK_____ NOT OK_____

13. P/S switch: OK_____ NOT OK_____

14. MAP: @ idle (park)_____ @ idle (drive)_____

15. MAF (grams/sec): @ idle (park)_____ @ idle (drive)_____

    @ 2,000 RPM (park)_____ @ key on (engine off)_____

16. IAC counts: @ idle (park)_____ @ idle (drive)_____

    @ A/C on (drive)_____ @ 2,000 RPM (park)_____

17. Throttle position (TP) sensor: @ idle_____ @ W.O.T. engine off, ignition "on"_____

18. Battery voltage:_____

19. Troubles with the vehicle? (if any)_____

DATE_____

_____   NAME_____

INSTRUCTOR'S OK

MAKE_____ MODEL_____ YR_____

GENERAL MOTORS DASH DATA RETRIEVAL WORKSHEET

(Not all of this data will be available on all vehicles or scan tools - if not available, put NA.)
To retrieve data from the instrument panel, press and hold the "off" and "warm" buttons until the display shows all segments. Answer the questions with blower "hi" button for yes and "low" button for no. (Use the service manual to interpret dash readings.)

1. Trouble codes: _____ PROM ID:_____

2. Engine coolant temperature (ECT): cold _____ warm _____

3. Intake air temperature (IAT):   cold _____ warm _____

4. Upstream O2S1:   lowest voltage observed _____ highest voltage observed _____

5. Upstream O2S2:   lowest voltage observed _____ highest voltage observed _____

6. Downstream O2S: lowest voltage observed _____ highest voltage observed _____

7. O_2 cross counts: @ idle____ @ 2,000 RPM____

8. Injector pulse width: @ idle (park)_____ @ idle (drive)_____

     @ 2,000 RPM (park)_____ @ 3,000 RPM (park)_____

9. Spark advance: @ idle (park)_____ @ idle (drive)_____

     @ 2,000 RPM (park)_____ @ 3,000 RPM (park)_____

10. Short term fuel trim (integrator): @ idle (park)_____

     @ idle (drive)_____ @ 2,000 RPM (park)_____

11. Long term fuel trim (block learn): @ idle (park)_____ @ idle (drive)_____

12. P/N switch: OK_____ NOT OK_____

13. P/S switch: OK_____ NOT OK_____

14. MAP: @ idle (park)_____ @ idle (drive)_____

15. MAF (grams/sec): @ idle (park)_____ @ idle (drive)_____

     @ 2,000 RPM (park)_____ @ key on (engine off)_____

16. IAC counts: @ idle (park)_____ @ idle (drive)_____

     @ A/C on (drive)_____ @ 2,000 RPM (park)_____

17. Throttle position (TP) sensor: @ idle_____ @ W.O.T. engine off, ignition "on"_____

18. Battery voltage:_____   DATE_____

_____   NAME_____

INSTRUCTOR'S OK

                              MAKE_____ MODEL_____ YR_____

"SUN MCA" DATA RETRIEVAL WORKSHEET

(Not all of this data will be available on all vehicles or scan tools - if not available, put NA.)

1. Trouble codes: _____ PROM ID:_____

2. Engine coolant temperature (ECT): cold _____ warm _____

3. Intake air temperature (IAT): cold _____ warm _____

4. Upstream O2S1: lowest voltage observed _____ highest voltage observed _____

5. Upstream O2S2: lowest voltage observed _____ highest voltage observed _____

6. Downstream O2S: lowest voltage observed _____ highest voltage observed _____

7. O_2 cross counts: @ idle____ @ 2,000 RPM____

8. Injector pulse width: @ idle (park)_____ @ idle (drive)_____

    @ 2,000 RPM (park)_____ @ 3,000 RPM (park)_____

9. Spark advance: @ idle (park)_____ @ idle (drive)_____

    @ 2,000 RPM (park)_____ @ 3,000 RPM (park)_____

10. Short term fuel trim (integrator): @ idle (park)_____

    @ idle (drive)_____ @ 2,000 RPM (park)_____

11. Long term fuel trim (block learn): @ idle (park)_____ @ idle (drive)_____

12. P/N switch: OK_____ NOT OK_____

13. P/S switch: OK_____ NOT OK_____

14. MAP: @ idle (park)_____ @ idle (drive)_____

15. MAF (grams/sec): @ idle (park)_____ @ idle (drive)_____

    @ 2,000 RPM (park)_____ @ key on (engine off)_____

16. IAC counts: @ idle (park)_____ @ idle (drive)_____

    @ A/C on (drive)_____ @ 2,000 RPM (park)_____

17. Throttle position (TP) sensor: @ idle_____ @ W.O.T. engine off, ignition "on"_____

18. Battery voltage:_____

19. Troubles with the vehicle? (if any)_____

                              DATE_____

_____

INSTRUCTOR'S OK

NAME_____

MAKE_____ MODEL_____ YR_____

"DRB II" DATA RETRIEVAL WORKSHEET

(Not all of this data will be available on all vehicles or scan tools - if not available, put NA.)

1. Trouble codes: _____ PROM ID:_____

2. Engine coolant temperature (ECT): cold _____ warm _____

3. Intake air temperature (IAT): cold _____ warm _____

4. Upstream O2S1: lowest voltage observed _____ highest voltage observed _____

5. Upstream O2S2: lowest voltage observed _____ highest voltage observed _____

6. Downstream O2S: lowest voltage observed _____ highest voltage observed _____

7. O_2 cross counts: @ idle____ @ 2,000 RPM____

8. Injector pulse width: @ idle (park)_____ @ idle (drive)_____

   @ 2,000 RPM (park)_____ @ 3,000 RPM (park)_____

9. Spark advance: @ idle (park)_____ @ idle (drive)_____

   @ 2,000 RPM (park)_____ @ 3,000 RPM (park)_____

10. Short term fuel trim (integrator): @ idle (park)_____

    @ idle (drive)_____ @ 2,000 RPM (park)_____

11. Long term fuel trim (block learn): @ idle (park)_____ @ idle (drive)_____

12. P/N switch: OK_____ NOT OK_____

13. P/S switch: OK_____ NOT OK_____

14. MAP: @ idle (park)_____ @ idle (drive)_____

15. MAF (grams/sec): @ idle (park)_____ @ idle (drive)_____

    @ 2,000 RPM (park)_____ @ key on (engine off)_____

16. IAC counts: @ idle (park)_____ @ idle (drive)_____

    @ A/C on (drive)_____ @ 2,000 RPM (park)_____

17. Throttle position (TP) sensor: @ idle_____ @ W.O.T. engine off, ignition "on"_____

18. Battery voltage:_____

19. Troubles with the vehicle? (if any)_____

DATE_____

INSTRUCTOR'S OK _____

NAME_____

MAKE_____ MODEL_____ YR_____

"DRB III" DATA RETRIEVAL WORKSHEET

(Not all of this data will be available on all vehicles or scan tools - if not available, put NA.)

1. Trouble codes: _____ PROM ID:_____

2. Engine coolant temperature (ECT): cold _____ warm _____

3. Intake air temperature (IAT): cold _____ warm _____

4. Upstream O2S1: lowest voltage observed _____ highest voltage observed _____

5. Upstream O2S2: lowest voltage observed _____ highest voltage observed _____

6. Downstream O2S: lowest voltage observed _____ highest voltage observed _____

7. O$_2$ cross counts: @ idle____ @ 2,000 RPM____

8. Injector pulse width: @ idle (park)_____ @ idle (drive)_____

    @ 2,000 RPM (park)_____ @ 3,000 RPM (park)_____

9. Spark advance: @ idle (park)_____ @ idle (drive)_____

    @ 2,000 RPM (park)_____ @ 3,000 RPM (park)_____

10. Short term fuel trim (integrator): @ idle (park)_____

    @ idle (drive)_____ @ 2,000 RPM (park)_____

11. Long term fuel trim (block learn): @ idle (park)_____ @ idle (drive)_____

12. P/N switch: OK_____ NOT OK_____

13. P/S switch: OK_____ NOT OK_____

14. MAP: @ idle (park)_____ @ idle (drive)_____

15. MAF (grams/sec): @ idle (park)_____ @ idle (drive)_____

    @ 2,000 RPM (park)_____ @ key on (engine off)_____

16. IAC counts: @ idle (park)_____ @ idle (drive)_____

    @ A/C on (drive)_____ @ 2,000 RPM (park)_____

17. Throttle position (TP) sensor: @ idle_____ @ W.O.T. engine off, ignition "on"_____

18. Battery voltage:_____

19. Troubles with the vehicle? (if any)_____

DATE_____

_____
INSTRUCTOR'S OK

NAME_____

MAKE_____ MODEL_____ YR_____

DATA RETRIEVAL AND DOWNLOAD WORKSHEET

Many hand-held scan tools such as the Tech 1, Tech 2 and DRB III can retrieve data from the vehicle and be downloaded into a larger computer for processing.

_____ 1. Retrieve the scan data from a snap shot from a vehicle.

_____ 2. Download the snap shot data into the host computer.

_____ 3. Select three parameters from the data list and graph the result. Show the instructor the graph.

       Instructor's okay: _____

_____ 4. Record the highest value of the following data captured:

       RPM _____

       IAC _____

       TP _____

DATE_____

UNIT 4

DIGITAL METERS AND SCOPES

_____
INSTRUCTOR'S OK

NAME_____

MAKE_____ MODEL_____ YR_____

GENERAL VOLTMETER TEST WORKSHEET

Connect the voltmeter red lead to the positive (+) post of the battery and the black lead to the negative (-) post of the battery. Set the scale of the voltmeter to read battery voltage. Turn the headlights on for 1 minute to remove the surface charge. Turn off the headlights and read the voltmeter.

_____ 1. Battery Voltage: 12.6 volts or higher = 100% charged
 12.4 volts   = 75% charged
 12.2 volts   = 50% charged
 12.0 volts   = 25% charged

Battery Voltage_____ OK____ NOT OK____

_____ 2. Cranking Voltage: Remove and ground the coil wire from the distributor or remove the power lead from the HEI (white clip) to prevent the engine from starting. While cranking the engine with the ignition key, observe the voltmeter. The voltage should be above 9.6 volts.

Cranking Voltage_____ OK____ NOT OK____

If at or below 9.6 volts, there is a possible problem with:
A. defective (or dirty) battery cables and connections.
B. defective (or discharged) battery (under load).
C. defective starter, solenoid or relay.

_____ 3. Charging Voltage: Reconnect the coil wire and start the engine. With the engine running at approximately 2,000 RPM (fast idle), the voltage should be 13.5-15 volts (or a minimum of 1/2 volt higher than battery voltage and a maximum of 2 volts higher than battery voltage).

Charging Voltage_____ OK____ NOT OK____

If over 15 volts, there is a possible defective voltage regulator or connections. If under 13.5 volts (or under 1/2 volt over battery voltage), there is a possible problem with:
A. loose alternator belt.
B. dirty or defective wiring connections.
C. defective voltage regulator.
D. defective alternator.

DATE_____

_____   NAME_____

INSTRUCTOR'S OK

MAKE_____ MODEL_____ YR_____

BRAKE SWITCH WORKSHEET

The brake switch activates the rear brake lights and acts as an input device for all of the following:

- **Speed (Cruise) Control** - when the brake pedal is depressed, the speed (cruise) control is turned off. If the brake switch is out of adjustment or defective, the speed (cruise) control may not work at all or continue to control the accelerator even when the brakes are applied.

- **Torque Converter Clutch** - when the brakes are applied, the torque converter clutch inside the automatic transmission/transaxle is disabled to permit engine braking during deceleration.

- **ABS Input** - when the brake pedal is depressed, the antilock braking system is signaled that a braking event has started.

_____ 1. Locate the brake switch (many vehicles use two or more switches).

_____ 2. With the key "on" (engine off) back probe both terminals of the brake switch and measure the DC volts at each.

_____ 3. With the brake pedal up (brake <u>not</u> applied) voltage should be measured on only the power side of the switch.

Voltage on the power side = _____ (should be close to the battery voltage)

Voltage on the load side = _____ (should be zero or close to zero)

_____ 4. Depress the brake pedal and measure the voltage at both terminals.

Voltage on the power side = _____ (should be close to battery voltage)

Voltage on the load side = _____ (should also be close to battery voltage)

_____ 5. Unplug the electrical connector from the brake switch and measure the resistance between the terminals.

Brake pedal up resistance (switch open) = _____ ohms (should be OL [infinity])

Brake pedal down resistance (switch closed) = _____ ohms (should be close to zero)

DATE_____

_____   NAME_____

INSTRUCTOR'S OK

MAKE_____ MODEL_____ YR_____

DIGITAL STORAGE SCOPE TESTING WORKSHEET

_____ 1. **Throttle position (TP) sensor (key on, engine off)** - move the throttle from idle
to wide open throttle (WOT) and back to idle:

volts per division = _____
time per division = _____
good _____ bad _____   why or why not? _____
Drawing of pattern:

_____
| |
| |
| |
| |
| |
|_____|

_____ 2. **Hall-effect or magnetic crankshaft or camshaft sensor:**

volts per division = _____
time per division = _____
good _____ bad _____   why or why not? _____
Drawing of pattern:

_____
| |
| |
| |
| |
| |
|_____|

_____ 3. **Fuel injector:**

volts per division = _____
time per division = _____
good _____ bad _____   why or why not? _____
Drawing of pattern:

_____
| |
| |
| |
| |
| |
|_____|

DATE_____

DIGITAL STORAGE SCOPE WAVEFORM ANALYSIS WORKSHEET

The purpose of this worksheet is to act as a checklist for the technician to use when diagnosing DSO waveforms.

_____ 1. Set the time/div to allow 2 to 4 patterns to be displayed except for potentiometer (TP sensor).

_____ 2. Set the volts/div to allow the entire anticipated waveform to be displayed both positive (+) and negative (-).

_____ 3. Set the trigger to positive or negative as dictated by the anticipated waveform.

_____ 4. Set the delay to minus 1, 2, or 3 to be assured that the entire waveform will be displayed in the center of the screen.

_____ 5. Look for the waveform to be within 0.6 V (600 mV) of ground if a ground-controlled component is being observed such as a fuel injector.

_____ 6. Look for sharp transitions when the voltage changes. Unevenness may indicate a deteriorated switching transistor circuit.

_____ 7. Look for consistency. If one or more patterns are not consistent with the other, waveforms indicate a problem.

   OK _____ NOT OK _____

   Why or why not? _____

   _____

   _____

   _____

DATE_____

NAME_____

MAKE_____ MODEL_____ YR_____

ECM GROUND WORKSHEET

A poor ECM ground can cause a variety of problems including reduced engine performance, false codes or SES light on and no codes.

_____ 1. Locate and drop the ECM.

_____ 2. Using the service manual, locate all ECM grounds. Record the circuit number and pin location for each:

	Circuit #	Terminal #	Voltage Drop
A.	_____	_____	_____
B.	_____	_____	_____
C.	_____	_____	_____

_____ 3. With the ignition "ON", the engine "OFF", measure the voltage drop between the ECM ground terminals and a good body ground.

      NOTE: Back probe the ECM terminals and use a
              <u>non-painted</u> body ground such as a door
              jam switch as a reference ground.

_____ 4. Record the voltage drop above (should be less than 0.20 volt):

        _____ **ALL OK**   _____ **ALL NOT OK**

_____ 5. Show the instructor the terminals tested and the service manual: _____ initials

DATE_____

NAME_____

INSTRUCTOR'S OK

MAKE_____ MODEL_____ YR_____

CHECK THE BLOWER FOR RADIO NOISE WORKSHEET

A digital meter set to read AC volts can be used to easily check the capacitor connected to the blower motor. A blower motor generates an AC voltage as it rotates. It is the purpose and function of the capacitor attached to the positive power lead to eliminate any potential radio noise that could be created by the blower motor. To check to see if the capacitor is okay, follow these easy steps:

_____ 1. Set a digital multimeter to read AC volts.

_____ 2. Use a T-pin and carefully back probe the power lead at the blower motor, being careful not to pierce the insulation. (The T-pin should just touch the metal terminal inside the plastic connection.)

_____ 3. Connect one lead (with AC volts, it doesn't matter which lead is connected to which terminal) to the T-pin and the other lead to a good engine or body ground.

_____ 4. Turn the blower on while observing the meter display. Check the AC voltage at all blower speeds.

Low   = _____
Medium   = _____
Medium high = _____
High   = _____

The capacitor, blower motor, and wiring are okay if the AC voltage is less than 0.5 volt (500 mV).

OK _____ NOT OK _____

DATE_____

UNIT 5

ADVANCED STARTING AND CHARGING SYSTEM DIAGNOSIS

INSTRUCTOR'S OK

NAME_____

MAKE_____ MODEL_____ YR_____

BATTERY LOAD TEST WORKSHEET

_____ 1. Connect the carbon pile tester per the test equipment manufacturer's instructions.

_____ 2. Determine the correct amount of load = _____ amps.

    A. 3 × amp/hour of the battery.
    B. 1/2 CCA of the battery.

_____ 3. Remove the surface charge by applying a load of 300 amps for 15 seconds. Let the battery recover for 30 seconds.

_____ 4. Apply load for 15 seconds. With the load still applied, read the battery voltage = _____ volts.

RESULTS: The battery voltage should be greater than 9.6 volts at the end of 15 seconds with the electrical load still applied. If the battery voltage is below 9.6 volts, recharge the battery and repeat the test. If the second test also indicates less than 9.6 volts, replace the battery.

NOTE: If testing a 6-volt battery, all procedures are the same except that the voltages stated should be divided by 2.

OK_____ NOT OK_____

DATE_____

NAME_____

MAKE_____ MODEL_____ YR_____

BATTERY CHARGING WORKSHEET

_____ 1. Measure the open-circuit voltage of the battery = _____ volts (red lead of the voltmeter to positive [+] and black lead to negative [-]).

(If more than 12.6 V, remove the surface charge by turning on the headlights for 1 minute).

_____ 2. % of charge = _____%.

12.6 V or higher = 100% charged
12.4 V   = 75% charged
12.2 V   = 50% charged
12.0 V   = 25% charged
below 11.9 V   = discharged

_____ 3. Determine the cold cranking amperes (CCA) of the battery = _____.

(The charge rate should be 1% of the CCA. For example, a battery with a 500 CCA rating should be charged at a 5 ampere rate.) Charge Rate = $\frac{CCA}{100}$

_____ 4. Determine the reserve capacity in minutes = _____.

(The charge rate can be determined by dividing the reserve capacity of the battery (in minutes) by 30. For example, a 180 minute battery should be charged at a 6 ampere rate - 180/30 = 6).
Charge Rate = $\frac{Reserve\ Capacity}{30}$

_____ 5. The battery should be charged @ _____ amperes (CCA method)

or @ _____ amperes (reserve capacity method).

DATE_____

NAME_____

MAKE_____ MODEL_____ YR_____

BATTERY ELECTRICAL DRAIN TEST WORKSHEET

Make certain all accessories are off and doors are closed before testing for battery drain. If battery drain is found, determine which circuit is causing the drain by disconnecting the fuses one at a time, until the drain is eliminated.

_____ 1. **AMMETER METHOD:**

    A. disconnect the negative (-) battery cable.

    B. connect the ammeter in series between the disconnected cable end and the battery negative terminal.

    C. read the ammeter.

    D. battery drain _____ amp. Normal parasitic load is 20-30 mA (0.02-0.03 A).

    Most vehicle manufacturers specify a maximum battery electrical draw of 50 mA (0.05A).

_____ 2. **TEST LIGHT METHOD:**

    A. disconnect the negative (-) battery cable.

    B. connect the test light to the negative battery cable and the negative battery terminal.

    C. test light should <u>not</u> light.

    D. results: ___ on bright ___ on dimly ___ off.

DATE_____

INSTRUCTOR'S OK

NAME_____

MAKE_____ MODEL_____ YR_____

PARASITIC DRAW TEST SWITCH WORKSHEET
(Using J-38758 Draw Test Switch)

_____ 1. Remove the battery cable from the battery negative terminal.

_____ 2. Install the parasitic draw test switch male end to the negative battery terminal.

_____ 3. Turn the test switch knob to the "off" position.

_____ 4. Install the negative battery cable to the female end of the test switch tool.

_____ 5. Turn the test switch tool knob to the "on" position.

_____ 6. Road test the vehicle while activating all accessories (radio, A/C, etc.).

_____ 7. Turn the ignition switch to the "locked" position and remove the ignition key.

_____ 8. Set the ammeter to the 10 amp scale and connect to the terminals on the test switch tool.

_____ 9. Turn the test switch tool knob to the "off" position to allow current to flow through the ammeter.

_____ 10. Check the current reading. If the current reading is at or below two amps, turn the test tool knob to the "on" position (to maintain continuity in the electrical system) and switch down to the two amp scale for a more accurate reading when the drain test tool knob is turned "off".

   NOTE: Always turn the test switch tool knob to the "on" position before removing each fuse to maintain continuity in the electrical system and to avoid damaging the ammeter due to accidental overloading (i.e. opening the door to change a fuse, etc.)

_____ 11. If the current draw is above specifications listed in the standby current load chart, remove the system fuses one fuse at a time until the current draw returns to less than .050 A (50 mA).

_____ 12. When cause of excessive current draw has been located and repaired, remove the current drain test tool and connect the negative battery cable to the negative battery terminal.   DATE_____

NAME_____

MAKE_____ MODEL_____ YR_____

CHRYSLER IGNITION OFF DRAW (IOD) TEST WORKSHEET

_____ 1. Locate the ignition off draw (IOD) fuse.

_____ 2. Disconnect the fuse and attach the leads from a digital multimeter set to read DC amperes.

CAUTION: When the meter leads are placed in the correct terminal of the meter, and one lead is connected to a powered circuit, the other lead has full battery voltage available because an ammeter allows full circuit current to flow through the meter. Hold the test leads of an ammeter away from any metal objects while testing to avoid possible damage to the vehicle and the meter.

_____ 3. Attach the leads of the meter to the terminals in the fuse panel where the fuse was located. Close the door(s) of the vehicle and observe the ammeter. The meter reading is the amount of ignition off draw.

IOD = _____A (normal draw is 20 to 30 mA (0.02-0.03 A)

OK _____ **NOT OK** _____

DATE_____

_____
INSTRUCTOR'S OK

NAME_____

MAKE_____ MODEL_____ YR_____

CRANKING CIRCUIT VOLTAGE-DROP TEST WORKSHEET

<u>DO 1 THROUGH 5 FOR EACH OF THE FOLLOWING TESTS</u>:

1. Set the voltmeter on the low scale.

2. Connect the red lead to the <u>most</u> positive.

3. Connect the black lead to the <u>most</u> negative.

4. Remove and ground the coil wire (or disconnect the "BAT" lead to GM HEI).

5. Crank the engine and observe the voltmeter.

<u>TESTS</u>:

_____ 1. Test the positive (+) battery cable connections = _____ volts. (<u>top post battery only</u>)

_____ 2. Test the negative (-) battery cable connections = _____ volts. (<u>top post battery only</u>)

_____ 3. Test the battery ground cable = _____ volts.

_____ 4. Test the positive (+) cable from the battery to the solenoid = _____ volts.

_____ 5. Test the solenoid between the "B" battery terminal and the "M" (motor) terminal = _____ volts.

RESULTS: **ALL OK _____**   **ALL NOT OK _____**

<u>Ford-type Cranking Circuit ONLY</u>:

Test the positive (+) cable from the relay to the starter = _____ volts.
Most vehicle manufacturers recommend a maximum voltage drop of 0.2 volt (200 mV) for any cable and a maximum voltage drop of 0.1 volt (100 mV) per connection.

DATE_____

NAME_____

MAKE_____ MODEL_____ YR_____

INSTRUCTOR'S OK
_____

NEUTRAL/CLUTCH SAFETY SWITCH WORKSHEET

_____ 1. Locate the neutral safety switch and explain its location on your vehicle.

Describe the location:

_____

_____ 2. Bypass the neutral/clutch safety switch and explain.

NOTE: MAKE SURE THE VEHICLE IS IN PARK OR NEUTRAL.

Color of the wires: _____

How was the switch bypassed? _____

_____ 3. Look up in a service manual and explain how to adjust the neutral/clutch safety switch.

Describe: _____

_____

_____

_____ 4. Draw the starter circuit for your make of vehicle and include:

    A. ignition switch
    B. relays
    C. solenoid
    D. neutral safety switches
    E. starter
    F. cables & wires
    G. battery

DATE_____

NAME_____

INSTRUCTOR'S OK

MAKE_____ MODEL_____ YR_____

STARTER AMPERAGE TEST WORKSHEET

_____ 1. Connect the starting and charging test leads per manufacturer's instructions.

_____ 2. Prevent the engine from starting (ground the coil wire or disconnect the "BAT" lead from HEI).

_____ 3. Crank the engine observing the ammeter scale (disregard the initial higher amp reading).

_____ 4. Starter amperage specifications for this vehicle = _____ amps.

        4 cylinder   - 150 A, maximum
        V-6   - 200 A, maximum
        V-8   - 250 A, maximum

    NOTE: Most vehicle manufacturers' specifications for starter amperage are for a starter being tested off the vehicle on a test bench.

_____ 5. Starter amperage test results = _____ amps.

    OK_____   NOT OK_____

    HINT: If the amperage reading is higher than the maximum allowable, double check the battery condition before removing the starter motor for disassembly, testing, or replacement. An engine problem can also cause an excessive amperage reading. If the amperage reading is within specifications (less than the maximum allowable), yet the starter motor is operating slowly, check for excessive resistance in the battery cables.

DATE_____

_____
INSTRUCTOR'S OK

NAME_____

MAKE_____ MODEL_____ YR_____

STARTING AND CHARGING TESTS WORKSHEET

_____ 1. General Voltmeter Test
      A. battery voltage = _____ (Remove the surface charge.)
      B. cranking voltage = _____ (Should be above 9.6 volts.)
      C. charging voltage = _____ (Should be 13.5=15.0 volts.)

_____ 2. Voltage-Drop Testing
      Connect the red voltmeter lead to the most positive (+).
      Connect the black voltmeter lead to the most negative (-).
      Crank the engine. (Voltage drop should not exceed 0.2 volt.)

      Voltage drop across the positive (+) cable(s) = _____.
      Voltage drop across the negative (-) cable = _____.
      Voltage drop across the solenoid   = _____.

_____ 3. Battery Load Test
      Load the battery to 1/2 CCA for 15 seconds.

      CCA = _____.   Load to = _____.
      Terminal voltage at the end of 15 seconds = _____.
      (Terminal voltage should be above 9.6 volts.)

_____ 4. Starter Amperage Test
      4 cylinders = 150 A, maximum. V-6 = 200 A, maximum.
      V-8 = 250 A, maximum.

      Cranking amps = _____. **OK_____ NOT OK_____**

_____ 5. Alternator Output Test
      At 2,000 engine RPM:

      _____amps tested _____amps specifications **OK____ NOT OK__**
      (Results should be within 10% of specifications.)

_____ 6. Charging System Requirement Test
      (Turn on all accessories, read the ammeter, add 5 A.)
      = _____ amps.

DATE_____

NAME_____

MAKE_____ MODEL_____ YR_____

INSTRUCTOR'S OK

AC RIPPLE VOLTAGE FROM THE ALTERNATOR WORKSHEET

A good alternator should <u>not</u> produce any AC voltage. It is the purpose of the diodes in the alternator to rectify all AC voltage into DC voltage.

_____ 1. Set the DVOM to read AC volts.

_____ 2. Start the engine and operate at 2,000 RPM (fast idle).

_____ 3. Connect the voltmeter leads to the positive (+) and negative (-) battery terminals @ battery.

_____ 4. Turn on the headlights to provide an electrical load on the alternator.

_____ 5. AC volts @ battery = _____. **OK_____ NOT OK_____**

_____ 6. Repeat the same test, but this time touch the red voltmeter lead to the output terminal of the alternator.

AC volts @ alternator = _____. **OK_____ NOT OK_____**

Was the reading higher @ the alternator?

YES_____ NO_____ WHY?_____

Results: If the diodes are good, the voltmeter should read <u>less</u> than 0.4 volt AC. If the reading is over 0.5 volt AC, the rectifier diodes are defective.

NOTE: This test will <u>not</u> test for a defective diode trio.

DATE_____

INSTRUCTOR'S OK

NAME_____

MAKE_____ MODEL_____ YR_____

SCOPE TESTING THE ALTERNATOR

Checking an alternator with a scope is an easy way to see if the diodes and/or stator inside the alternator are functioning correctly.

_____ 1. Connect the scope probe lead to the output terminal of the alternator.

_____ 2. Connect the scope probe ground lead to a good vehicle ground or to the **rear** housing of the alternator.

_____ 3. Set the scope settings as follows:

> Volts Per Division = 100 mV AC
> Time Per Division = 500 μS (500 microseconds)
> Trigger Level   = 50 mV AC (50%)
> Trigger Slope   = positive (+)

_____ 4. Start the engine and turn on the headlights to create an electrical load for the alternator. Observe the scope pattern.

_____ 5. Regular, even ripples indicate that the alternator is okay. Irregularities of the ripples indicate a problem and could cause electrical interference that can cause radio noise.

> Draw the waveform here:

OK _____ **NOT OK** _____

DATE_____

NAME_____

MAKE_____ MODEL_____ YR_____

CHARGING SYSTEM VOLTAGE DROP WORKSHEET

_____ 1. Connect the DVOM set to read DC volts to the alternator output terminal and the positive (+) of the battery.

_____ 2. Start the engine and run to 2,000 RPM (fast idle).

_____ 3. Turn on the headlights to force the alternator to charge the battery.

_____ 4. The voltage drop reading should not exceed 0.40 volt (400 mV).

     _____ = the voltage drop of the <u>insulated</u> (power side) of the charging circuit.

                  OK_____ NOT OK_____

_____ 5. To test if the alternator is properly grounded, continue operating the engine at a fast idle with the lights on, connect the meter leads to the case of the alternator and the negative (-) terminal of the battery. A reading of greater than 0.20 volt (200 mV) indicates a poor alternator ground.

     _____ = the voltage drop of the <u>ground side</u> of the alternator.

                  OK_____ NOT OK_____

DATE_____

INSTRUCTOR'S OK
_____

NAME_____

MAKE_____ MODEL_____ YR_____

ALTERNATOR OUTPUT TEST WORKSHEET

_____ 1. Connect the starting and charging test leads per the manufacturer's instructions.

_____ 2. Turn the ignition switch on and observe the ammeter.
   Ignition current = _____amps.

_____ 3. Start the engine and operate at 2,000 RPM (fast idle).

_____ 4. Turn the load increase control slowly to obtain the highest reading on the ammeter scale. (Do not let the battery voltage drop to less than 12 volts.)
   Tested amps = _____ amps.

_____ 5. Total amps (add #2 and #4 results) = _____ amps.

_____ 6. Specification (should be stamped on the alternator or indicated by a colored tag on or near the output terminal) = _____ amps.

_____ 7. Results should be within 10% of the specifications. If the alternator amperage output is low, first check the condition of the alternator drive belt. The alternator should not be able to be rotated by hand with the engine off.

   OK_____   NOT OK_____

DATE_____

NAME_____

MAKE_____ MODEL_____ YR_____

STARTING/CHARGING TEST USING MIN/MAX WORKSHEET

Using the "MIN/MAX" feature of a digital multimeter makes testing the starting and charging system easy.

_____ 1. Set the digital multimeter to read DC volts. Select "AUTO" range or manually set the scale to read up to at least 20 volts.

_____ 2. Connect the red meter test lead to the positive terminal of the battery and the black meter test lead to the negative terminal of the battery.

_____ 3. Select MIN/MAX on the meter.

_____ 4. Crank and start the engine and allow the meter to read for 15 seconds to allow the alternator to start to charge the battery.

_____ 5. Retrieve the minimum (MIN) and maximum (MAX) reading from the meter. (See the instruction manual for your meter for details.)

        MAX reading = _____ (it should be 13.5 - 15.0 volts)

          OK _____ **NOT OK** _____

        MIN reading = _____ (it should be above 9.6 volts)

          OK _____ **NOT OK** _____

DATE_____

_____
INSTRUCTOR'S OK

NAME_____

MAKE_____ MODEL_____ YR____

STARTING AND CHARGING SYSTEM DIAGNOSIS WITH A SCAN TOOL WORKSHEET

The starting and charging system can be easily checked using a scan tool on any vehicle where the data stream is available and the appropriate scan tool for the vehicle is used.

_____ 1. Connect the scan tool to the data link connector (DLC) of the vehicle.

_____ 2. Set the scan tool to read the battery voltage.

> **NOTE:** The scan tool displays the voltage reading taken from the vehicle computer. This may not be the same voltage as measured at the battery, but it represents the voltage the computer is monitoring. The voltage difference between the computer and the measured value at the battery should not exceed 0.5 volt.

_____ 3. Observe and record the battery voltage:

before cranking the engine = _____V (it should be 12.4 V or higher)

during engine cranking = _____ V (it should be above 9.6 V)

with the engine running = _____ V (it should be 13.5 - 15.0 V)

> **HINT:** To make this recording even easier, use the "snap shot" capability of the scan tool and record the starting event. Scroll through the data stream frames one at a time and record the voltage. Looking at engine speed (RPM) will indicate when the engine was being cranked (80 - 250 RPM) or running (over 400 RPM).

DATE_____

SCAN TOOL TESTING OF BATTERY VOLTAGE

A scan tool displays voltage readings that are received by the computer. It is possible that the battery voltage, cranking voltage and charging voltage are within specifications when measured at the battery, but may not be okay according to the computer.

_____ 1. Connect a scan tool to the data link connector (DLC).

_____ 2. Connect a digital multimeter set to read DC volts to the positive (+) and negative (-) terminals of the battery.

_____ 3. Turn the ignition to on (engine off) and observe the scan tool voltage and the meter voltage.

        Voltage read by the scan tool = _____ volts

        Voltage read by the meter = _____ volts

_____ 4. Start the engine and hold the RPM to 2000 while observing both the scan tool and the meter.

        Voltage read by the scan tool = _____ volts (should be 13.5-15.0)

        Voltage read by the meter = _____ volts (should be 13.5-15.0)

        (The above should be within 0.2 volts of each other.)

If the voltage difference is greater than 0.2 difference, check for poor electrical

connections in the computer wiring or high resistance in the computer ground(s).

Maximum voltage drop of a computer ground should be 0.2 volts.

DATE_____

_____   NAME_____

INSTRUCTOR'S OK

MAKE_____ MODEL_____ YR_____

LIGHTER PLUG VOLTAGE WORKSHEET

The lighter plug is "HOT at all times" in many vehicles. The electrical power to the plug comes from the battery through a fusible link and through a lighter fuse usually located in the fuse panel. The lighter plug is a convenient location to check battery voltage, cranking voltage, and charging voltage without having to lift the hood or gain access to the battery. All measurements can be performed using a lighter plug with wires attached to a digital multimeter.

_____ 1. Connect the lighter plug into the lighter socket and connect it to the multimeter. Set the meter to read DC volts.

Battery voltage = _____ (should be above 12.6 volts due to possible surface charge).
Turn on the headlights and watch the voltmeter until the voltage stabilizes and then turn the headlights off and wait until the voltage again stops rising. The battery voltage with the surface charge removed = _____ volts (should be 12.4 volts or higher). **OK _____ NOT OK _____**

_____ 2. Crank the engine while observing the voltmeter.

Cranking voltage = _____ volts (should be above 9.6 volts).
OK _____ NOT OK _____

_____ 3. Start the engine and operate it at a fast idle (about 2,000 RPM) and note the charging system voltage = _____ volts (should be 13.5-15.0 volts)
OK _____ NOT OK _____

_____ 4. Switch to AC voltage with the engine running. Turn on the headlights to provide an electrical load.

AC ripple voltage = _____ volts (should be less than 0.4 volt).
OK _____ NOT OK _____

_____ 5. If the meter is equipped with MIN/MAX record, repeat steps 1, 2 and 3 while recording the voltages.

MAX = _____ volts (should be 13.5-15.0 volts) **OK _____ NOT OK _____**
MIN = _____ volts (should be above 9.6 volts) **OK _____ NOT OK _____**

DATE_____

NAME_____

MAKE_____ MODEL_____ YR_____

ALTERNATOR FUSIBLE LINK CHECK WORKSHEET

Alternators produce electrical power to supply the electrical needs of the vehicle and to keep the battery fully charged. The output terminal of the alternator (usually labeled "B" or "BAT") connects to the positive (+) terminal of the battery through a fusible link. The purpose of the fusible link is to protect the electrical system from a possible fire if the alternator happened to short to ground. If the wire or alternator is shorted to ground, all electrical energy available in the battery could overheat the connecting wiring unless a fusible link is present to open the circuit.

To check that the fusible link is not melted (open), use the following methods:

Method #1 - Connect a 12-volt test light to a good body or chassis ground and touch the test light probe to the output terminal of the alternator. The test light <u>should</u> light.

OK ____ NOT OK ____

Method #2 - Connect the red lead of a voltmeter to the output terminal of the battery and the black lead to the case of the alternator. The meter should read battery voltage (about 12.6 volts).

OK ____ NOT OK ____

DATE _____

NAME_____

MAKE_____ MODEL_____ YR_____

ALTERNATOR DRIVE BELT INSPECTION WORKSHEET

The alternator drive belt must be in serviceable condition and at the proper tension to transmit engine power to the alternator. A loose or defective drive belt (often called an **accessory drive belt**) can prevent the alternator from producing its maximum-rated output.

_____ 1. A thorough visual inspection should be performed. Check for cracks on the pulley side of the belt. The maximum allowable number of cracks are three in three inches on any one rib.

   Number of cracks in 3 inches = _____

   OK _____   **NOT OK** _____

_____ 2. Check the position of the belt tensioner. Most tensioners have a reference mark to indicate the range where the belt should be operating to be assured of proper tension.

   OK _____   **NOT OK** _____

HINT: If the belt(s) is noisy, use a water spray bottle and spray the belts with a fine mist of water while the engine is running. If the noise goes away temporarily, then returns when the water evaporates, the belt is the source of the noise. If the noise does not change, then further testing is needed to locate the component that is the source of the noise.

DATE _____

NAME_____

INSTRUCTOR'S OK

MAKE_____ MODEL_____ YR_____

ALTERNATOR REQUIREMENT WORKSHEET

The purpose and function of this test is to provide a fast and easy method to determine if the alternator (AC generator) is capable of providing an adequate amount of charging current.

_____ 1. Connect the carbon pile tester (such as a VAT-40) to the battery.

_____ 2. Attach the current probe around all of the positive (+) or negative (-) battery cables (which ever is easiest to attach).

_____ 3. Set the tester to read charging amperes.

_____ 4. Start the engine and allow it to operate until normal operating temperature is achieved.

_____ 5. Raise the engine speed to a fast idle (about 2000 RPM) and start turning on every electrical device that could normally be turned on such as:

      A. the heater blower on high speed
      B. the windshield wipers on high speed
      C. the headlights on high (brights)
      D. the brake lights
      E. the radio or sound system

_____ 6. Observe and record the ammeter reading = _____ amperes (should be a positive (+) number over 5 amperes). In other words, the alternator should be capable of supplying all of the current necessary to operate all of the electrical components plus a minimum of 5 amperes.

      OK _____   **NOT OK** _____

DATE_____

UNIT 6

IGNITION SYSTEM DIAGNOSIS

NAME_____

_____
INSTRUCTOR'S OK

MAKE_____ MODEL_____ YR_____

MEGGER TEST WORKSHEET

The purpose of this test is to find defective or fouled spark plugs without having to remove them from the engine.

_____ 1. Set the ohmmeter to the highest range (should be higher than 10 megohms [10 million ohms] or 10 MΩ).

_____ 2. Remove the spark plug wire from the spark plug, being careful not to damage the plug wire. Grab the wire by the boot (the portion of the plug wire covering the spark plug) and gently twist and pull to remove the wire from the plug.

_____ 3. Touch one end of the ohmmeter to the center terminal of the spark plug and the other end to a good clean engine ground or the negative (-) terminal of the battery.

_____ 4. Results = _____ (should be infinity).

The ohmmeter should not show any reading, but rather indicate an open (lack of continuity). On digital meters this is usually indicated by a solid or flashing "1" or "3" or the letters "OL" meaning over-limit.

If the ohmmeter indicates any reading other than an open circuit, this indicates that the spark plug is fouled by carbon deposits or is cracked or otherwise defective.

OK_____ NOT OK_____

NOTE: If this test indicates other than OL on the ohmmeter, there is a definite problem. However, the spark plug could still be fouled and not be indicated by this test.

DATE_____

NAME _____

MAKE_____ MODEL_____YR_____

SPARK PLUG WIRE TESTING WORKSHEET

_____ 1. Set the ohmmeter to <u>KΩ</u> scale.

.

_____ 2. List the length in feet and the resistance values in ohms for each spark plug wire according to the cylinder number:

<u>Length (feet)</u>   <u>Ohms</u>

1. _____   _____

2. _____   _____

3. _____   _____

4. _____   _____

5. _____   _____

6. _____   _____

7. _____   _____

8. _____   _____

Coil wire: _____   _____

_____ 3. Results - TV-RS wires should test 10,000 ohms (10KΩ) or <u>less</u> per foot of length.

OK_____   NOT OK_____

DATE_____

_____
INSTRUCTOR'S OK

NAME _____

MAKE_____ MODEL_____ YR_____

SPARK PLUGS WORKSHEET

_____ 1. Determine the correct plug code and gap for your vehicle using a spark plug application guide. Also check other guides or the cross-over interchange section of the guide for two other brand name codes:

ENGINE: #cylinders_____ VIN#_____

BRAND_____ BRAND_____ BRAND_____

CODE#_____ CODE#_____ CODE #_____

GAP _____ GAP _____ GAP _____

_____ 2. Remove and label all the spark plug wires.

_____ 3. Determine the condition and gap of all spark plugs:

<u>Condition</u>   <u>Gap</u>

1. _____ _____
2. _____ _____
3. _____ _____
4. _____ _____
5. _____ _____
6. _____ _____
7. _____ _____
8. _____ _____

_____ 4. Reinstall the spark plug (start by hand).

NOTE: Use an anti-seize compound on the threads of the spark plugs being installed into aluminum cylinder heads.

_____ 5. Use a torque wrench and torque the spark plugs to the proper torque.

Specified torque = _____

_____ 6. Start the engine. Check for possible rough running caused by crossed or loose spark plug wires.

OK_____ NOT OK_____

DATE_____

INSTRUCTOR'S OK

NAME_____

MAKE_____ MODEL_____ YR_____

DISTRIBUTOR CAP AND ROTOR INSPECTION WORKSHEET

_____ 1. Carefully remove the distributor cap (the spark plug wires do not have to be removed from the cap).

_____ 2. Determine the **locating tab** on the distributor cap.

_____ 3. Check the **towers** for corrosion by removing one spark wire from the cap at a time.

_____ 4. Check the **center carbon insert** for chips or cracks.

_____ 5. Check the **side inserts** inside the cap for excessive corrosion and dusting.

_____ 6. Check the cap for **cracks** or **carbon tracks** inside and out.

_____ 7. Check the condition of the **rotor**.

OK_____ NOT OK_____

DATE_____

_____
INSTRUCTOR'S OK

NAME_____

MAKE_____ MODEL_____ YR_____

IGNITION COIL TEST WORKSHEET

_____ 1. Set the ohmmeter on the low scale.

_____ 2. Using a service manual, look up the correct specifications for the ignition coil.

   Specifications: primary_____ secondary_____

_____ 3. For best, most accurate results, disconnect all wires from the coil.

_____ 4. Measure the resistance between the two primary winding terminals = _____ ohms.

   (Normal resistance for most coils = 1 - 3 ohms.)
   Check for the exact specifications if the test
   results do not fall within the above range.

   NOTE: Many high energy electronic ignition systems use coils with less than 1
         ohm in the primary winding.

      OK_____   NOT OK_____

_____ 5. Set the ohmmeter to read a maximum of 30,000 ohms.

   NOTE: Most analog ohmmeters should be recalibrated every time the ohmmeter
         scale is switched.

   Measure the resistance between either primary terminal and the secondary tower.

_____ 6. Secondary winding resistance = _____ ohms.

   (Normal specifications usually range between 6000 - 30,000 ohms.)

      OK_____   NOT OK_____

                              DATE_____

_____
INSTRUCTOR'S OK

NAME_____

MAKE_____ MODEL_____ YR____

IGNITION COIL HIGH RESISTANCE CHECKS WORKSHEET

Ignition coils can be tested for any high-resistance conductive paths.

1. Check for paths that may exist between the secondary winding and the primary coil winding. (This test will indicate a non-intentional electrical path and is designed to test ignition coils without an internal connection.)

   HINT: If the coil has four terminals including the output terminal, there is no internal connection.

2. Check that the secondary winding does not have a high-resistance path to ground caused by tracking or carbon tracks.

Ohms Check:

_____ 1. Disconnect all wiring from the ignition. (This assures that the measurement will involve only the ignition coil itself and not other components of the ignition circuit.)

_____ 2. Set the meter to read high resistance (400 megohm scale).

_____ 3. To check for a high-resistance path to ground, connect one meter lead to the coil output terminal (high voltage terminal) and the other to the metal laminations of the coil or a good chassis ground. Ohmmeter reading = _____ (should be OL)

_____ 4. To check for a high-resistance path between the primary and secondary coil windings, connect one meter lead to the coil output terminal and the other lead to one of the primary coil winding terminals. Ohmmeter reading = _____ (should be OL)
      OK _____ **NOT OK** _____

Nanosiemens Check:

Nanosiemens is the unit of measure for electrical conductance which is the inverse of resistance. To connect nanosiemens (nS) to megohms (1,000,000 Ω), divide the reading into 1,000. For example, a reading of 2nS converts to 500 mΩ (1000 ÷ 2). Set the meter to read nS.

_____ 1. To check the secondary coil winding conductance to ground, connect one meter lead to the coil output terminal and the other meter lead to a good chassis ground or the steel laminations of the coil. Reading = _____ (should be less than 2.5 nS)

_____ 2. To check for conductance between the primary and secondary windings of the coil, connect one meter lead to the coil output terminal and the other meter lead to one of the primary coil winding terminals. Reading = _____ (should be less than 2.5 nS)
      OK _____ **NOT OK** _____   DATE_____

_____ NAME_____

INSTRUCTOR'S OK

MAKE_____ MODEL_____ YR_____

IGNITION TIMING WORKSHEET

_____ 1. Perform all pre-timing checks (1 through 6 below).

_____ 2. Timing specifications: _____BTDC at _____RPM.

_____ 3. Timing was at _____BTDC.

OK_____   NOT OK_____

_____ 4. According to a service manual, what had to be done before checking the ignition timing? _____

HOOK-UP AND PROCEDURE:

_____ 1. Connect the power to the timing light according to the manufacturer's directions (usually to + and - of the battery).

_____ 2. Hook the inductive pickup to the #1 cylinder near the distributor.

_____ 3. Chalk the timing marks.

_____ 4. Remove and plug the vacuum hose at the distributor, if required. Computer-equipped engines require exact timing procedures. Consult the underhood decal for timing information.

_____ 5. The engine should be warm and at the correct timing RPM.

_____ 6. If the timing is incorrect, loosen the nut at the bottom of the distributor (base) and rotate the distributor until the timing marks line up.

_____ 7. Tighten the distributor hold down and recheck the timing.

_____ 8. Reinstall the vacuum lines or set timing connections.

DATE_____

NAME_____

MAKE_____ MODEL_____ YR_____

_____
INSTRUCTOR'S OK

ELECTRONIC IGNITION TESTING WORKSHEET

_____ 1. Pickup coil specifications = _____ ohms.

_____ 2. Pickup coil tested result = _____ ohms.
(except Hall-effect)

OK_____ NOT OK_____

_____ 3. Crank the engine with the pickup coil disconnected from the module and the meter connected to the pickup coil leads (set the meter to "AC volts") = _____ AC volts (should be higher than 0.25 volts AC).

_____ 4. Test the module by turning the ignition "on" (RUN) with the engine "off", and hold a 110-volt soldering gun near the distributor cap (to induce a moving magnetic field in the pickup coil). The module is good if a spark occurs out of the coil.

OK_____ NOT OK_____

DATE_____

INSTRUCTOR'S OK _____

NAME _____

MAKE_____ MODEL_____ YR_____

ELECTRONIC IGNITION (DISTRIBUTORLESS) ANALYSIS WORKSHEET

_____ 1. Identify the type of distributorless ignition you are working with:

      _____ A. Magnavox (Type I) (one coil pack for 6 cylinders)

      _____ B. AC Delco (Type II) (3 individual replaceable coils)

      _____ C. Ford

      _____ D. Chrysler

      _____ Other

_____ 2. What type of triggering system is used to signal the ignition module?

      _____

_____ 3. Test the coils for output by unplugging both plug wires from one coil (Type II) and start the engine. Does a spark occur between the secondary electrodes?

      _____

_____ 4. Repeat #3 for the other coils. Do they all spark correctly?

      _____

_____ 5. Install 2" lengths of vacuum hose between the coil terminals and spark plug wire. Using a test light, ground out one cylinder at a time.

      A. Did all cylinders drop in RPM when grounded? _____

         If not, which cylinder did not drop in RPM? _____

      B. If a cylinder RPM does not drop when the plug wire is grounded, what items could be defective?

         _____

      C. By grounding out one spark plug wire, does it ground out one or two cylinders? _____

                                      DATE_____

NAME _____

MAKE_____ MODEL_____ YR_____

IGNITION OSCILLOSCOPE TESTING WORKSHEET

_____ 1. Connect the red clamp on the #1 cylinder spark plug wire (operates the tach and timing light).

_____ 2. Connect the silver clamp on the coil wire (HEI adapter on the HEI distributor cap top) (scope pattern).

_____ 3. Connect the red small lead from the blue wire coil connector to the negative (-) side of the coil (tach terminal).

_____ 4. Connect the small black lead from the blue wire coil connector to a good engine ground.

_____ 5. Record the firing line height from _____ to _____ KV.

_____ 6. Record the length of spark lines _____
       (should be 4 - 7 degrees or 1.0 - 2.0 ms).

_____ 7. Record the number of intermediate oscillations _____.

_____ 8. Check for the fuel mixture imbalance (alternating high, low firing lines).

OK _____   NOT OK _____

_____ 9. Record the dwell at idle as shown on the scope _____.

_____10. Record the dwell at 2,000 RPM as shown on the scope _____.

_____11. Snap accelerate the engine. All firing lines should rise the same. If one or more fail to rise, this indicates a fouled spark plug. List the cylinder(s) not rising

_____.

DATE_____

NAME _____

_____
INSTRUCTOR'S OK

MAKE_____ MODEL_____ YR_____

DISTRIBUTOR TESTING WORKSHEET

This worksheet can be done using a distributor machine and testing the distributor out of the vehicle. Follow manufacturer's procedures.

The test results can also be obtained by using a set-back (timing advance) type timing light.

_____ 1. Distributor number _____.

_____ 2. Distributor rotation direction? _____

_____ 3. Mechanical advance <u>specifications</u>:

      _____ degrees _____ at RPM   _____ degrees _____ at RPM
      _____ degrees _____ at RPM   _____ degrees _____ at RPM

_____ 4. Vacuum advance <u>specifications</u>:

      start at _____ in. Hg
      _____ degrees at _____ in. Hg
      _____ degrees at _____ in. Hg
      _____ degrees at _____ in. Hg

_____ 5. Mechanical advance <u>results</u>:

      _____ degrees _____ at RPM   _____ degrees _____ at RPM
      _____ degrees _____ at RPM   _____ degrees _____ at RPM

_____ 6. Vacuum advance <u>results</u>:

      start at _____ in. Hg
      _____ degrees at _____ in. Hg
      _____ degrees at _____ in. Hg
      _____ degrees at _____ in. Hg

_____ 7. Describe the corrections needed to obtain a correct distributor reading:

_____
_____
_____

DATE_____

INSTRUCTOR'S OK _____

NAME _____

MAKE_____ MODEL_____ YR_____

GLITCH CAPTURE WORKSHEET
(GM Vehicle Only)

Most General Motors computerized engines use four wires between the ignition module (distributor or DIS module) and the computer. These four wires and their color include:

White -   Electronic spark timing (EST) signal from the computer to the ignition module.

Purple -   RPM reference signal from the crankshaft position sensor or pickup coil to the computer.

Tan (Brown)- Bypass signal from the computer to the ignition module.

Black -   Ground. This lead assures that the ignition module ground and the computer ground are connected and both electrically connected to a good clean engine ground.

Operation - Whenever the computer senses an engine speed greater than 400 RPM, 5 volts DC are applied to the ignition module to transfer timing control from the module to the computer. If something happens to the computer power or ground, the 5 volts on the bypass wire will drop to zero (0) then back to 5 volts. By monitoring the 5 volts bypass signal, a glitch can be captured.

_____ 1. Connect a digital meter such as a Fluke 87 set to read DC volts and min/max record at the 1 mS setting. A digital storage scope (DSO) can also be used.

_____ 2. T-pin the tan (brown) bypass wire at a convenient location (usually near the ignition module or distributor [if so equipped]).

_____ 3. Start the engine and confirm the presence of 5 volts on the bypass circuit.

_____ 4. Very quickly cycle the ignition key to off, then on again fast enough to allow the engine to stumble without stalling.

_____ 5. Check the min. reading - a zero (or very low voltage) reading indicates that the glitch was captured. A drop in the voltage line to within 0.6 (600 mV) of zero (ground) indicates that the glitch was captured on the scope.

OK ____ NOT OK ____

DATE_____

NAME_____

_____
INSTRUCTOR'S OK

MAKE_____ MODEL_____ YR_____

BEAR ACE WORKSHEET

_____ 1. Determine the primary circuit information:

    A. primary current _____ amps.

    B. primary voltage drop _____ .

_____ 2. Determine the secondary circuit information:

	Firing KV	Burn KV	Burn Time	Delta KV
cyl. #1	_____	_____	_____	_____
cyl. #2	_____	_____	_____	_____
cyl. #3	_____	_____	_____	_____
cyl. #4	_____	_____	_____	_____
cyl. #5	_____	_____	_____	_____
cyl. #6	_____	_____	_____	_____
cyl. #7	_____	_____	_____	_____
cyl. #8	_____	_____	_____	_____

_____ 3. Determine the 4-gas information:

	HC	CO	CO_2	O_2
at idle:	_____	_____	_____	_____
at 2,000 RPM:	_____	_____	_____	_____

_____ 4. Alternator scope pattern. Draw the pattern:

DATE_____

_____
INSTRUCTOR'S OK

NAME_____

MAKE_____ MODEL_____ YR_____

ALLEN SMART SCOPE WORKSHEET

_____ 1. Determine the primary circuit information:

    A. primary current _____ amps.

    B. primary voltage drop _____.

_____ 2. Determine the secondary circuit information:

	Firing KV	Burn KV	Burn Time	Delta KV
cyl. #1	_____	_____	_____	_____
cyl. #2	_____	_____	_____	_____
cyl. #3	_____	_____	_____	_____
cyl. #4	_____	_____	_____	_____
cyl. #5	_____	_____	_____	_____
cyl. #6	_____	_____	_____	_____
cyl. #7	_____	_____	_____	_____
cyl. #8	_____	_____	_____	_____

_____ 3. Determine the 4-gas information:

	HC	CO	CO_2	O_2
at idle:	_____	_____	_____	_____
at 2,000 RPM:	_____	_____	_____	_____

_____ 4. Alternator scope pattern. Draw the pattern:

DATE_____

_____

INSTRUCTOR'S OK

NAME_____

MAKE_____ MODEL_____ YR_____

SCAN TOOL TESTING OF THE IGNITION SYSTEM WORKSHEET

A scan tool can be used to monitor what the vehicle computer is looking at and what commands are being sent to the various engine actuators and components.

_____ 1. Connect the scan tool to the data link connector (DLC) of the vehicle.

_____ 2. Scroll through the various parameters until engine RPM and ignition spark timing can be viewed.

   Idle RPM = _____

   Spark advance at idle = _____

_____ 3. Slowly increase engine speed and observe the amount of spark advance.

   Spark advance at 1000 RPM = _____ degrees

   Spark advance at 1500 RPM = _____ degrees

   Spark advance at 2000 RPM = _____ degrees

   Spark advance at 2500 RPM = _____ degrees

_____ 4. Scroll the display of the scan tool until knock sensor (KS) activity or timing retard is displayed (if the vehicle is so equipped).

   KS signal at idle = _____ (should be zero) (The engine should not have detected an engine knock.)

_____ 5. Increase engine speed while observing KS or timing retard amount. Did the computer retard timing?

   Yes _____ no _____

_____ 6. Lightly tap on the engine block and observe KS or timing retard with the engine warmed above idle speed. Was a knock detected?

   Yes _____ No _____

                                        DATE_____

NAME_____

_____
INSTRUCTOR'S OK

MAKE_____ MODEL_____ YR_____

OPTICAL DISTRIBUTOR SCOPE TEST WORKSHEET

Many vehicles such as the Chevrolet (LT1, V-8) or the Nissan Maxima (3.0L, V-6), use an optical distributor. Optical distributors use a rotor disk with holes that separate light emitting diodes (LEDs) from optical pickup. The slits are different sizes and shapes. High resolution slits are generally spaced so that one slit represents 1° of crankshaft rotation. Another row of slits may differ in size and represent each cylinder (6 slits for a V-6 engine or 8 slits for a V-8 engine).

_____ 1. Locate and carefully back probe, using T-pins, the low resolution and high resolution signal wires at a connector near the distributor. (Refer to the factory service manual for the correct connector and color of the wires.)

_____ 2. Connect the scope probe lead to one of the T-pins and connect the probe ground lead to a good engine ground.

_____ 3. Set the scope settings as follows:

        Volts per Division = 2 volts DC
        Time per division = 500 μS (500 microseconds)
        Trigger Level   = 1 V. (50%)
        Trigger Slope   = positive (+)

_____ 4. Start the engine and observe the waveform. The waveform should have vertical rising and falling edges and the ground signal (horizontal bottom portion of the waveform) should be close to zero volts. Draw the waveform here:

        OK _____   NOT OK _____

_____ 5. Connect the scope to the high resolution signal wire. Carefully verify that all rising and falling edges are vertical and that the ground signal should be close to zero. Draw the waveform here:

        OK _____   NOT OK _____

                                   DATE_____

NAME_____

INSTRUCTOR'S OK

MAKE_____ MODEL_____ YR____

MAGNETIC SENSOR SCOPE TEST WORKSHEET

Magnetic sensors are used by many vehicle manufacturers as crankshaft position sensors, camshaft position sensors, and wheel speed sensors. All magnetic sensors contain a magnet surrounded by a coil of wire. When a notched wheel passes near the magnet, the magnetic field strength changes. This changing magnetic field causes a changing voltage in the coil windings.

_____ 1. Locate the magnetic sensor to be tested and carefully back probe the sensor pigtail connector using a T-pin.

_____ 2. Connect the scope probe lead to the T-pin and connect the probe ground lead to a good engine ground.

_____ 3. Set the scope settings as follows:

       Volts per Division = 5 volts AC
       Time per Division = 500 milliseconds (5 ms)
       Trigger Level   = 2 volts AC (50%)
       Trigger Slope   = positive (+)

_____ 4. Start the engine and observe the scope pattern.
     The highest voltage of a peak = _____ volts. Draw the waveform here:

OK _____ NOT OK _____

DATE_____

NAME_____

MAKE_____ MODEL_____ YR_____

FORD PIP AND SPOUT DUAL-TRACE SCOPE WORKSHEET

Ford computers control dwell time (coil saturation time) by charging the coil on-time. As the engine speed increases, the dwell is increased to permit a larger interval for the coil to be charged. This increase can be observed on a scope by connecting to the SPOUT signal wire.

_____ 1. Draw the PIP signal at idle speed.

_____ 2. Draw the PIP signal at 2500 RPM.

_____ 3. Draw the SPOUT signal at idle speed.

_____ 4. Draw the SPOUT signal at 2500 RPM.

_____ 5. If using a dual-trace oscilloscope, draw both the PIP and SPOUT @ idle and 2500 RPM and illustrate the timing advance.

DATE_____

NAME_____

MAKE_____ MODEL_____ YR_____

INSTRUCTOR'S OK

HALL-EFFECT SENSOR SCOPE TEST WORKSHEET

Hall-effect sensors are used by many vehicle manufacturers for crankshaft position or camshaft position. Most Hall-effect sensors use three wires - a power, signal, and ground wire.

_____ 1. Locate the Hall-effect sensor to be tested. Carefully back probe the signal wire at the sensor pigtail connector using a T-pin. (Refer to the factory service manual for the exact location of the sensor and signal wire.)

_____ 2. Connect the scope probe lead to the T-pin and connect the probe ground lead to a good engine ground.

_____ 3. Set the scope settings as follows:

       Volts per Division = 5 volts DC
       Time per Division = 10 milliseconds (10 ms)
       Trigger Level   = 1 volt AC (50%)
       Trigger Slope   = positive (+)

_____ 4. Start the engine and observe the scope pattern. The waveform should have straight vertical rising and falling edges and the ground portion of the signal (horizontal bottom portion of the waveform) should be close to zero volts.

Draw the waveform as displayed here:

OK _____ NOT OK _____

DATE_____

UNIT 7

ENGINE FUELS AND DRIVEABILITY DIAGNOSIS

_____
INSTRUCTOR'S OK

NAME_____

MAKE_____ MODEL_____ YR_____

ALCOHOL IN GASOLINE TEST WORKSHEET

Take the following steps when testing gasoline for alcohol content:

_____ 1. Pour suspect gasoline into a small clean beaker or glass container.

DO NOT SMOKE OR PERFORM THIS TEST AROUND SOURCES OF IGNITION

_____ 2. Carefully fill the graduated cylinder to the 10 ml mark.

_____ 3. Add 2 ml of water to the graduated cylinder by counting the number of drops from the eye dropper. (Before performing the test, the eye dropper must be calibrated to determine how many drops equal 2.0 ml.)

_____ 4. Put the stopper in the cylinder and shake vigorously for 1 minute. Relieve built-up pressure by occasionally removing the stopper. Alcohol dissolves in water and will drop to the bottom of the cylinder.

_____ 5. Place the cylinder on a flat surface and let it stand for 2 minutes.

_____ 6. Take a reading near the bottom of the cylinder at the boundary between the two liquids.

_____ 7. For percent of alcohol in gasoline, subtract 2 from the reading and multiply by 10.

For example: The reading is 3.1 ml: $3.1 - 2 = 1.1 \times 10 = 11\%$ alcohol

The reading is 2.0 ml: $2 - 2 = 0 \times 10 = 0\%$ alcohol (no alcohol)

If the increase in volume is 0.2% or less, it may be assumed that the test gasoline contains no alcohol. What is the percentage of alcohol in the sample? _____%

DATE_____

INSTRUCTOR'S OK

NAME_____

MAKE_____ MODEL_____ YR_____

REID VAPOR PRESSURE TEST WORKSHEET

When testing the RVP of gasoline, take the following steps:

_____ 1. Rinse the inside of the fuel cup.

_____ 2. Fill the insulated cup with hot water (about 110°F) to within ¾ in. of full.

_____ 3. Using a chilled syringe (or dropper), withdraw chilled gasoline from the sample bottle and fill the fuel cup within 1/8 in. of the top.

_____ 4. Let it stand for at least two minutes. Tap the gauge lightly while reading the pressure.

_____ 5. Using the pressure and temperature as read, refer to the correction table in Appendix 3 to obtain the gasoline vapor pressure corrected to 100°F.

RVP of sample = _____.

DATE_____

UNIT 8

COMPUTER SENSOR TESTING

INSTRUCTOR'S OK

NAME_____

MAKE_____ MODEL_____ YR____

OXYGEN SENSOR DIAGNOSIS WORKSHEET

(Digital Voltmeter Method)

_____ 1. Locate the oxygen sensor(s) and carefully back probe the sensor wire at a connector with a "T" pin.

_____ 2. Attach the red lead of the digital voltmeter to the sensor and ground the black meter lead to a good clean non-painted ground.

_____ 3. Start the engine and allow it to run at 2500 RPM for 2 minutes to get the oxygen sensor up to operating temperature and get the engine into closed loop.

_____ 4. Select MIN/MAX record and maintain the engine speed at 2500 RPM for 2 additional minutes.

   Record the   MIN _____   MAX _____   AVERAGE _____

_____ 5. Results: MIN should be below 200 mV and MAX should be above 800 mV. The average should be about 450 mV.

   A. If the average is higher than 450 mV, the engine is operating with a rich air-fuel mixture.
   B. If the average is lower than 450 mV, the engine is operating with a lean air-fuel mixture.

OK _____ NOT OK _____

DATE_____

INSTRUCTOR'S OK

_____

NAME_____

MAKE_____ MODEL_____ YR_____

OXYGEN SENSOR DIAGNOSIS WORKSHEET

(Scan Tool Method)

_____ 1. Connect the scan tool to the DLC and start the engine.

_____ 2. Operate the engine at a fast idle (2500 RPM) for 2 minutes to allow time for the oxygen sensor to warm to operating temperature.

_____ 3. Observe the oxygen sensor activity on the scan tool to verify closed loop operation.

_____ 4. Select "snap shot" mode and hold the engine speed steady and start recording.

_____ 5. Play back snap shot and place a mark beside each range of oxygen sensor voltage for each frame of the snap shot.

Between 0 and 300 mV   Between 300 and 600 mV   Between 600 and 1000 mV

_____   _____   _____
(record # of times)   (record # of times)   (record # of times)

_____ 6. Results: A good oxygen sensor and computer system should result in most snap shot values at both ends (0 to 300 and 600 to 1000 mV). If most of the readings are in the middle, the oxygen sensor is not working correctly.

OK _____   **NOT OK** _____

DATE_____

NAME_____

MAKE_____ MODEL_____ YR_____

OXYGEN SENSOR DIAGNOSIS WORKSHEET

(Scope Analysis Method)

_____ 1. Locate the oxygen sensor(s) and carefully back probe the sensor wire at a connector with a "T" pin.

_____ 2. Attach the scope probe to the oxygen sensor signal wire. Connect the ground wire from the scope probe to a good engine ground.

_____ 3. Start the engine and allow it to run at 2500 RPM for 2 minutes to allow the oxygen sensor to reach operating temperature and the engine to achieve closed loop operation.

_____ 4. Select the proper time base and volts per division (try 200 mS per division and 200 mV per division).

_____ 5. Observe the scope pattern:

  A. What is the highest voltage observed? _____ Max. volts

  B. What is the lowest voltage observed? _____ Min volts

  C. How many times does the voltage cycle in one second? _____
      (Should be 0.5 to 5.0 Hz.)

      OK _____   NOT OK _____

DATE_____

NAME_____

MAKE_____ MODEL_____ YR_____

O₂ SENSOR CLEANING WORKSHEET

NOTE: This procedure only works with fuel-injected engines.

_____ 1. Name of assistant: _____

_____ 2. Start the engine and allow it to get into closed loop operation.

_____ 3. Using a frequency counter (meter) or scan tool, determine the O_2 cross counts @ 2000 RPM: cross counts_____   **OK_____ NOT OK_____**

_____ 4. Unplug the O_2 sensor connector.

_____ 5. Install the jumper wire into the wiring harness side (ECM side) of the O_2 wiring <u>only</u>.

             CAUTION: Do not connect the jumper wire to the O_2 sensor - the sensor can be <u>destroyed</u>.

_____ 6. Start the engine and operate it at a fast idle (2000 RPM).

_____ 7. Using your body, apply voltage to the O_2 sensor wire. (After licking your fingers, touch the positive (+) post of the battery with one hand and the jumper wire terminal with the other.)

_____ 8. Observe the engine operation. (It is normal for the engine to stumble slightly due to the lean condition formed by the high O_2 voltage.) Use an assistant to maintain the engine speed if necessary.

_____ 9. Do not operate the engine for more than 1 minute (20-30 seconds on a warm engine is usually all the time necessary to clean the O_2 sensor).

_____ 10. Stop the engine. Restore the wire harness connector to the O_2 sensor and start the engine.

_____ 11. Determine the O_2 cross counts @ 2000 RPM: _____.

_____ 12. Change: _____

DATE_____

NAME_____

MAKE_____ MODEL_____ YR_____

GM PRESSURE SENSOR WORKSHEET

_____ 1. Identify type(s) of pressure sensor(s)

> _____ **BARO** (barometric pressure sensor) (blue connector) a signal to the ECM to change as vehicle changes altitude. Absolute pressure sensor usually located in the passenger compartment.

> _____ **MAP** (manifold absolute pressure sensor) (connector color varies with application:
> A. green - fuel injection
> B. red - carbureted engine (Buick engines)
> C. orange - turbocharged carbureted engines

> _____ **VAC** (vacuum sensor) gray connector.

_____ 2. Use a T-pin and carefully backprobe the signal wire at the connector. Connect a DVOM set to DC volts and connect the red meter lead to the T-pin and attach the black meter lead to a good chassis ground.

_____ 3. VAC sensor voltage at high vacuum = _____   (should have low voltage
                        at low vacuum = _____   at low vacuum)

MAP sensor voltage at high vacuum = _____   (should have high voltage
                        at low vacuum = _____   at low vacuum)

BARO sensor voltage at high vacuum = _____   (should have high voltage
                    at atmospheric pressure   = _____   at low vacuum)

_____ 4. Sensor(s) **OK** _____   **NOT OK** _____

DATE_____

INSTRUCTOR'S OK

NAME_____

MAKE_____ MODEL_____ YR_____

MAP SENSOR DIAGNOSIS WORKSHEET

Manifold absolute pressure (MAP) sensors detect engine load by measuring intake manifold vacuum relation to absolute zero pressure (a perfect vacuum inside the sensor).

_____ 1. Perform a thorough visual inspection including:

   A. Check the condition of vacuum hose.
   B. Check that the vacuum hose routing does not have any dips or sags in the vacuum hose between the sensor and the intake manifold.

   NOTE: A dip or low portion in the vacuum hose can create a trap where liquid fuel (condensed gasoline fumes) or water (condensed steam) can accumulate and block the vacuum signal to the MAP sensor.

   C. Disconnect the vacuum hose (if equipped) from the MAP sensor. If anything such as a liquid or other substance comes out of the sensor or the hose, replace the MAP sensor. Reconnect the vacuum hose to the MAP.

_____ 2. Turn the ignition key on (engine off), read and record the MAP sensor voltage (or frequency) = _____ volts (Hz) (use either a scan tool or digital meter connected to the signal wire). (Should be about 4.60 to 4.80 volts or 156-159 Hz.)

   OK _____ NOT OK _____

_____ 3. Start the engine and operate until normal operating temperature is achieved. Read and record the MAP sensor voltage (or Hz) at idle speed = _____volts (Hz). (Should be between 0.9 and 1.6 volts (102-109 Hz) if the engine varies between 17 and 21 inches of Hg.)

   OK _____ NOT OK _____

DATE_____

NAME_____

MAKE_____ MODEL_____ YR_____

MAP SENSOR GRAPH WORKSHEET

Most vehicle MAP sensors use a 5-volt reference, a signal return and a ground connection. As the vacuum inside the intake manifold changes, the MAP sensor voltage changes.

- High vacuum (low absolute manifold pressure) = low voltage
- Low vacuum (high absolute manifold pressure) = high voltage

_____ 1. Connect a T-pin to the signal wire connector at the MAP sensor.

_____ 2. Connect the red lead of a digital voltmeter set to read DC volts to the T-pin. Connect the black meter lead to a good chassis ground.

_____ 3. Disconnect the vacuum hose from the MAP sensor (or remove the sensor from the manifold) and attach a hand-operated vacuum pump to the sensor.

_____ 4. Place a dot on the graph that represents the MAP sensor voltage when 5, 10, 15, 20, 25 and 30 in. Hg of vacuum is applied to the sensor.

_____ 5. Connect the dots. The results should be a straight line.

OK _____ NOT OK _____

M A P   V O L T S

4.5
4.0
3.5
3.0
2.5
2.0
1.5
1.0
0.5
0

5   10   15   20   25   30

VACUUM APPLIED (in. Hg)

DATE _____

NAME_____

INSTRUCTOR'S OK

MAKE_____ MODEL_____ YR_____

GM MAP SENSOR DIGITAL METER WORKSHEET

A GM MAP sensor uses an electronic circuit that changes resistance as the engine vacuum changes. The charging resistance causes the 5-volt reference from the computer to change.

_____ 1. Locate the MAP sensor.
_____ 2. Connect the red lead of a digital multimeter to the signal output terminal by carefully back probing the connector with a T-pin. (Consult the factory service manual for the exact wiring harness color code for the vehicle which you are testing.)
_____ 3. Unplug the vacuum hose from the MAP sensor. Connect a hand-operated vacuum pump to the MAP sensor vacuum hose connection.
_____ 4. Set the digital multimeter to read DC volts.
_____ 5. Turn the ignition on (engine off) to supply power to the MAP sensor.
_____ 6. Using the hand-operated vacuum pump, record the volts at each 1 inch of Hg of vacuum applied to the sensor.

Vacuum (inches Hg)	GM (volts)
0	4.80
1	4.52
2	4.46
3	4.26
4	4.06
5	3.88
6	3.66
7	3.50
8	3.30
9	3.10
10	2.94
11	2.76
12	2.54
13	2.36
14	2.20
15	2.00
16	1.80
17	1.62
18	1.42
19	1.20
20	1.10
21	0.88
22	0.66

_____ 7. Does the voltage change smoothly with increasing vacuum? YES ___ NO ___
_____ 8. Compare these readings with the specifications for the vehicle being tested. Are the readings within specifications? YES _____ NO _____

DATE_____

NAME_____

MAKE_____ MODEL_____ YR_____

GM MAP SENSOR SCOPE TEST WORKSHEET

A GM MAP sensor uses an electronic circuit that changes resistance as the engine vacuum changes. The charging resistance causes the 5-volt reference from the computer to change.

_____ 1. Locate the MAP sensor.

_____ 2. Connect the red lead of a digital multimeter to the signal output terminal by carefully back probing the connector with a T-pin. (Consult the factory service manual for the exact wiring harness color code for the vehicle which you are testing.)

_____ 3. Unplug the vacuum hose from the MAP sensor. Connect a hand-operated vacuum pump to the MAP sensor vacuum hose connection.

_____ 4. Set the digital multimeter to read DC volts.

_____ 5. Turn the ignition on (engine off) to supply power to the MAP sensor.

_____ 6. Using the hand-operated vacuum pump, record the volts at each 1 inch of Hg of vacuum applied to the sensor.

Vacuum (inches Hg)	GM (volts)
0	4.80
1	4.52
2	4.46
3	4.26
4	4.06
5	3.88
6	3.66
7	3.50
8	3.30
9	3.10
10	2.94
11	2.76
12	2.54
13	2.36
14	2.20
15	2.00
16	1.80
17	1.62
18	1.42
19	1.20
20	1.10
21	0.88
22	0.66

_____ 7. Does the frequency change smoothly with increasing vacuum? **YES** ___ **NO** ___

_____ 8. Compare these readings with the specifications for the vehicle being tested. Are the readings within specifications? **YES** _____ **NO** _____

DATE_____

NAME_____

_____
INSTRUCTOR'S OK

MAKE_____ MODEL_____ YR_____

FORD MAP SENSOR DIGITAL METER WORKSHEET

A Ford MAP sensor uses a variable capacitor that changes in capacitance as the vacuum inside the capacitor changes. The electronic circuits inside the sensor convert the changing capacitance into a signal frequency that is proportional to the change in sensor capacitance.

_____ 1. Locate the MAP sensor.

_____ 2. Connect the red lead of a digital multimeter to the signal output terminal by carefully back probing the connector with a T-pin. The signal wire usually has the color green on the wire itself. (Consult the factory service manual for the exact wiring harness color code for the vehicle which you are testing.)

_____ 3. Unplug the vacuum hose from the MAP sensor. Connect a hand-operated vacuum pump to the MAP sensor vacuum hose connection.

_____ 4. Set the digital multimeter to read frequency (hertz [Hz.]).

_____ 5. Turn the ignition on (engine off) to supply power to the MAP sensor.

_____ 6. Using the hand-operated vacuum pump, record the frequency in Hertz at each 1 inch of Hg of vacuum applied to the sensor.

Vacuum (inches Hg)	Ford (Hz)
0	156-159
5	141-143
10	127-130
15	114-117
18	109
20	102-104

_____ 7. Does the frequency change smoothly with increasing vacuum? **YES** ___ **NO** ___

_____ 8. Compare these readings with the specifications for the vehicle being tested. Are the readings within specifications? **YES** _____ **NO** _____

DATE_____

INSTRUCTOR'S OK

NAME_____

MAKE_____ MODEL_____ YR____

FORD MAP SENSOR SCOPE TEST WORKSHEET

A Ford MAP sensor uses a variable capacitor that changes in capacitance as the vacuum inside the capacitor changes. The electronic circuits inside the sensor convert the changing capacitance into a signal frequency that is proportional to the change in sensor capacitance.

_____ 1. Locate the MAP sensor.

_____ 2. Connect the red lead of a digital scope to the signal output terminal by carefully back probing the connector with a T-pin. The signal wire usually has the color green on the wire itself. (Consult the factory service manual for the exact wiring harness color code for the vehicle which you are testing.)

_____ 3. Unplug the vacuum hose from the MAP sensor. Connect a hand-operated vacuum pump to the MAP sensor vacuum hose connection.

_____ 4. Set the digital scope to read frequency (hertz [Hz.]).

_____ 5. Turn the ignition on (engine off) to supply power to the MAP sensor.

_____ 6. Using the hand-operated vacuum pump, record the frequency at each 1 inch of Hg of vacuum applied to the sensor.

Vacuum (inches Hg)	Ford (Hz)
0	156-159
5	141-143
10	127-130
15	114-117
18	109
20	102-104

_____ 7. Does the frequency change smoothly with increasing vacuum? **YES** ___ **NO** ___

_____ 8. Compare these readings with the specifications for the vehicle being tested. Are the readings within specifications? **YES** _____ **NO** _____

DATE_____

INSTRUCTOR'S OK

NAME_____

MAKE_____ MODEL_____ YR_____

TEMPERATURE SENSORS WORKSHEET

_____ 1. Locate the engine coolant temperature (ECT) sensor used by the engine computer.

Wire colors = _____ and _____.

_____ 2. Locate and identify these coolant temperature sensors and list their wire color(s) in the blanks below:

A. sensor for dash "hot" light = _____.

B. sensor for dash temperature gauge = _____.

C. sensor for electric cooling fan = _____.

D. sensor for cold start injector on some fuel injected engines _____.

E. sensor for intake air temperature (IAT) = _____.
(may be located in the air cleaner)

DATE_____

NAME________________________________

____
INSTRUCTOR'S OK

MAKE________ MODEL________ YR_____

ENGINE COOLANT TEMPERATURE (ECT) GRAPH WORKSHEET

Most engine coolant temperature sensors (ECTs) use a negative temperature coefficient (NCT) thermistor. The resistance of the sensor decreases as the temperature of the engine coolant increases. The vehicle computer applies a voltage to the sensor. The purpose of this worksheet is to plot the relationship of the ECT sensor temperature and the voltage.

_____ 1. T-pin the signal wire of the engine coolant temperature (ECT) sensor.

_____ 2. Set the digital multimeter to read DC volts.

_____ 3. Connect a scan tool or use a pyrometer to measure engine coolant temperature.

_____ 4. Plot the voltage of the ECT every 10° as the engine warms up.

NOTE: Many engine computers connect another resistor in the ECT circuit when the temperature of the coolant reaches 120°-140°. This causes the voltage at the ECT sensor to rise, then continue to fall as the coolant temperature continues to rise.

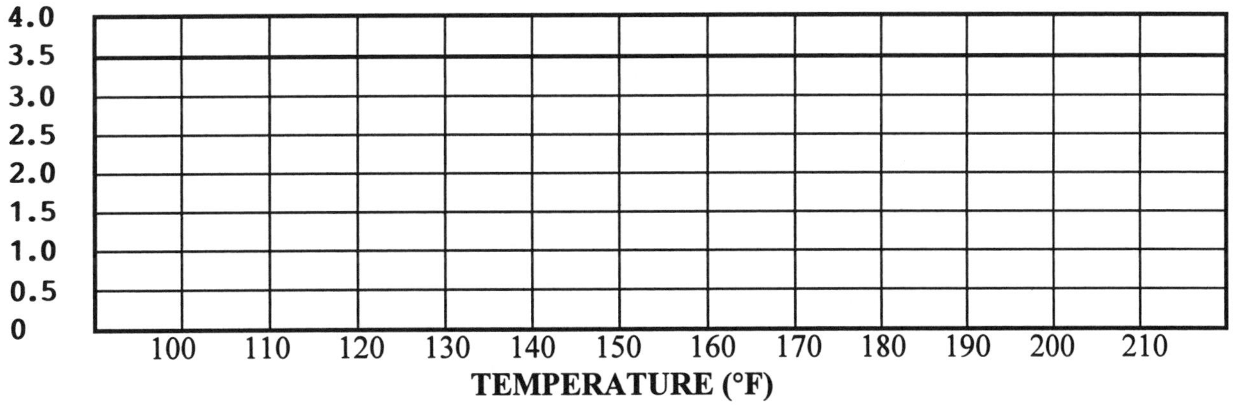

_____ 5. Was there a upward movement of the graph when the thermostat opened?

YES ____ **NO** ____

_____ 6. Was there a slight movement upward when the cooling fan came on?

YES ____ **NO** ____

DATE____________________

NAME_____

INSTRUCTOR'S OK

MAKE_____ MODEL_____ YR_____

ENGINE COOLANT TEMPERATURE (ECT) SENSOR WORKSHEET

(General Motors vehicles)

_____ 1. Locate the engine coolant temperature (ECT) sensor.

_____ 2. Wire colors for the sensor = _____ and _____.

_____ 3. Insert "T" pins into both electrical terminals.

_____ 4. Connect a DVOM to both terminals of the ECT and measure the voltage = _____V.

_____ 5. Compare voltage to the chart and estimate the engine coolant temperature = _____°F.

_____ 6. Based on the chart below, is the coolant temperature sensor:

OK _____   NOT OK _____

°C	°F	OHMS	VOLTAGE DROP ACROSS SENSOR
-40	-40	∞ to 100 K	4.95
- 8	18	14628	4.68
0	32	9420	4.52
10	50	5670	4.25
20	68	3520	3.89
30	86	2238	3.46
40	104	1459	2.97
50	122	973	2.47
60	140	667	2.00
70	158	467	1.59
80	176	332	1.25
90	194	241	0.97
100	212	177	0.75

DATE_____

_____
INSTRUCTOR'S OK

NAME_____

MAKE_____ MODEL_____ YR_____

ENGINE COOLANT TEMPERATURE (ECT) SENSOR WORKSHEET
(Chrysler vehicles ('81 - '84)

_____ 1. Locate the engine coolant temperature (ECT) sensor.

_____ 2. Wire colors for the sensor = _____ and _____.

_____ 3. Insert "T" pins into both electrical terminals.

_____ 4. Connect a DVOM to both terminals of the ECT and measure the voltage = _____ V.

_____ 5. Compare voltage to the chart and estimate the engine coolant temperature = _____ °F.

_____ 6. Based on the chart below, is the coolant temperature sensor: **OK ___ NOT OK ___**

Resistance: 70° F (21° C) - 7,000 - 13,000 Ω

200° F (93° C) -   400 - 1,500 Ω

Temperature ° F (° C)	Voltage (V)
-4 (-20)	3.28
14 (-10)	3.19
32 (0)	3.05
50 (10)	2.86
68 (20)	2.61
77 (25)	2.46
86 (30)	2.31
104 (40)	1.98
122 (50)	1.65
140 (60)	1.34
158 (70)	1.07
176 (80)	0.84
194 (90)	0.66
212 (100)	0.51
230 (110)	0.4
248 (120)	0.32

DATE _____

INSTRUCTOR'S OK
_____

NAME_____

MAKE_____ MODEL_____ YR_____

ENGINE COOLANT TEMPERATURE (ECT) SENSOR WORKSHEET
(Chrysler vehicles 1985 to current)

_____ 1. Locate the engine coolant temperature (ECT) sensor.

_____ 2. Wire colors for the sensor = _____ and _____.

_____ 3. Insert "T" pins into both electrical terminals.

_____ 4. Connect a DVOM to both terminals of the ECT and measure the voltage = _____V.

_____ 5. Compare voltage to the chart and estimate the engine coolant temperature = _____°F.

_____ 6. Based on the chart below, is the coolant temperature sensor: **OK** ___ **NOT OK** ___

Cold curve without pull-up resistor inside the ECM.

Temperature ° F (° C)	Voltage (V)
-20 (-30)	4.70
-10 (-25)	4.57
0 (-18)	4.45
10 (-12)	4.30
20 (- 7)	4.10
30 (- 1)	3.90
40 (4)	3.60
50 (10)	3.30
60 (16)	3.00
70 (21)	2.75
80 (27)	2.44
90 (32)	2.15
100 (38)	1.83
110 (43)	1.57
120 (49)	1.25

DATE_____

INSTRUCTOR'S OK
_____

NAME_____

MAKE_____ MODEL_____ YR_____

ENGINE COOLANT TEMPERATURE (ECT) SENSOR WORKSHEET

(Chrysler)

_____ 1. Locate the engine coolant temperature (ECT) sensor.

_____ 2. Wire colors for the sensor = _____ and _____.

_____ 3. Insert "T" pins into both electrical terminals.

_____ 4. Connect a DVOM to both terminals of the ECT and measure the voltage = _____V.

_____ 5. Compare voltage to the chart and estimate the engine coolant temperature = _____°F.

_____ 6. Based on the chart below, is the coolant temperature sensor:

OK _____ **NOT OK** _____

Hot curve with pull-up resistor inside the ECM.

Temperature ° F (° C)	Voltage (V)
130 (54)	3.77
140 (60)	3.60
150 (66)	3.40
160 (71)	3.20
170 (77)	3.02
180 (82)	2.80
190 (88)	2.60
200 (93)	2.40
210 (99)	2.20
220 (104)	2.00
230 (110)	1.80
240 (116)	1.62
250 (121)	1.45

DATE_____

INSTRUCTOR'S OK

NAME_____

MAKE_____ MODEL_____ YR_____

ENGINE COOLANT TEMPERATURE (ECT) SENSOR WORKSHEET

(Ford)

_____ 1. Locate the engine coolant temperature (ECT) sensor.

_____ 2. Wire colors for the sensor = _____ and _____.

_____ 3. Insert "T" pins into both electrical terminals.

_____ 4. Connect a DVOM to both terminals of the ECT and measure the voltage = _____V.

_____ 5. Compare voltage to the chart and estimate the engine coolant temperature = _____°F.

_____ 6. Based on the chart below, is the coolant temperature sensor:

OK _____ **NOT OK** _____

Temperature ° F (° C)	Resistance (Ω)	Voltage (V)
50 (10)	58,750	3.52
68 (20)	37,300	3.06
86 (30)	24,270	2.26
104 (40)	16,150	2.16
122 (50)	10,970	1.72
140 (60)	7,600	1.35
158 (70)	5,370	1.04
176 (80)	3,840	0.80
194 (90)	2,800	0.61
212 (100)	2,070	0.47
230 (110)	1,550	0.36
248 (120)	1,180	0.28

DATE_____

NAME_____

MAKE_____ MODEL_____ YR_____

THROTTLE POSITION (TP) SENSOR WORKSHEET

(Scope Method)

_____ 1. Locate the TP sensor.

_____ 2. Connect the jumper test leads between the harness connector and the sensor or carefully back probe the wires at the connector using T-pins.

_____ 3. Connect the probe ground wire to the ground wire of the sensor.

_____ 4. Connect the probe to the 5-V reference wire and turn the ignition switch to on (engine off).

_____ 5. Read the reference voltage on the scope = _____V.

_____ 6. Connect the probe to the signal wire and read the voltage on the scope with a closed throttle = _____V.

_____ 7. Slowly depress the accelerator pedal and watch for an even rise of voltage as the throttle is depressed.

NOTE: Avoid using your hand to open the throttle from under the hood. Using an assistant to depress the accelerator pedal duplicates the forces on the TP sensor during normal operation.

OK _____ **NOT OK** _____

DATE _____

_____
INSTRUCTOR'S OK

NAME_____

MAKE_____ MODEL_____ YR_____

THROTTLE POSITION (TP) SENSOR WORKSHEET

(Digital Meter Method)

_____ 1. Locate the throttle position (TP) sensor.

_____ 2. Connect the jumper test leads between the harness connector and the sensor or carefully back probe the wires at the connector using "T" pins.

_____ 3. Turn the ignition on (engine off).

_____ 4. Measure the reference voltage (gray wire) (should be close to 5 volts) = _____.

_____ 5. Measure the sensor voltage at idle _____,

specification = _____.

_____ 6. Measure TP sensor at W.O.T. = _____ volts.

_____ 7. Use the MIN/MAX setting of the voltmeter.

NOTE: Manually set the volt scale to 40 V to prevent a false "OL" when the meter automatically switches scales at 4 volts.

With the engine off, but the ignition "on" (run), carefully observe the voltmeter and raise the throttle opening slowly to W.O.T. and return to idle. There should not be any open or break in the voltmeter readings while moving the throttle.

OK _____ **NOT OK** _____

DATE_____

INSTRUCTOR'S OK
_____

NAME_____

MAKE_____ MODEL_____ YR_____

THROTTLE POSITION (TP) GRAPH WORKSHEET

The engine computer supplies a 5 volt reference voltage to the variable resistance throttle position sensor. At idle, the throttle position voltage as measured by the output of the TP sensor should be about 0.5 volt and about 4.5 volts when the throttle is in the wide open position.

_____ 1. Connect a T-pin to the sensor terminal of the TP sensor.

_____ 2. Connect the red lead of a digital meter set to read DC volts to the T-pin and the black lead to a good chassis ground.

_____ 3. Turn the ignition switch to on (engine off) and record the TP voltage at idle, ¼ throttle, ½ throttle, ¾ throttle and wide open throttle (WOT).

_____ 4. Place a dot at each point on the graph at idle, ¼, ½, ¾, and WOT. Connect the dots. The results should be a straight line.

OK _____ NOT OK _____

DATE_____

_____
INSTRUCTOR'S OK

NAME_____

MAKE_____ MODEL_____ YR_____

SENSOR TESTING WORKSHEET

_____ 1. Test the pickup coil or crankshaft position sensor with the ohmmeter = _____ ohms.
Specification = _____ **OK** _____ **NOT OK** _____

_____ 2. Test the pickup coil or crankshaft position sensor with the digital multimeter on the AC volt scale.
The AC volts with the engine cranking = _____ volts.
(Should be greater than 0.25 V) **OK** _____ **NOT OK** _____

_____ 3. Connect the scope leads to the pickup coil or crankshaft position sensor and crank the engine. Draw the scope pattern:

_____ 4. Connect the scope to a TP sensor. Turn the ignition "on" (engine off).

_____ 5. Observe the scope as the throttle is depressed and released. Draw the waveform.

    A. voltage at idle = _____ V.

    B. voltage at WOT = _____ V.

    C. check for smooth waveform without any opens or spikes downward that can indicate a short to ground. **OK** _____ **NOT OK** _____

_____ 6. Test a magnetic crankshaft sensor on the scope during cranking. Draw the pattern:

_____ 7. Test a Hall-effect sensor on the scope during cranking. Draw the pattern:

DATE_____

NAME_____

MAKE_____ MODEL_____ YR_____

INSTRUCTOR'S OK
_____

MAF SENSOR DIAGNOSIS GRAPH WORKSHEET

A "Mass Air Flow" sensor produces a variable output depending on the MASS of the air flow through the sensor. A faulty MAF can cause driveability problems and stalling. A good MAF sensor should produce a signal that increases with engine speed. This change should be linear, meaning that a line drawn through the points of engine RPM and frequency should be a straight line. Use either method A or B:

A. Use a meter or scope with a frequency counter to record frequency at least every 200 RPM increase in engine speed from idle to 2,000 RPM.

B. Use a scan tool and record grams per second at every 100 RPM increase in engine speed from idle to 2,000 RPM.

_____ 1. Plot grams/sec. Or frequency on the graph at various engine RPMs.

	150
	140
Frequency	130
(HZ)	120
	110
or	100
	90
Grams per	80
sec.	70
(G/S)	60
	50
	40
	30
	20
	10
	0

Idle   - Engine Speed -   2,000

_____ 2. The results should be a straight line. Any drop outs or spikes could indicate a faulty MAF sensor.

OK _____ NOT OK _____

DATE_____

NAME_____

MAKE_____ MODEL_____ YR_____

MAF SENSOR SCOPE WORKSHEET

Most mass air flow sensors produce a variable frequency signal proportional to the amount (mass) of air flowing through the sensor.

_____ 1. Locate the MAF sensor and connect the scope probe to the signal wire on the sensor by carefully back probing the connector using a T-pin.

_____ 2. Connect the scope probe ground lead to a good non-painted engine or body ground.

_____ 3. Draw the MAF sensor signal at idle speed with the engine in neutral or park.

_____ 4. Place the gear selector in drive or reverse (automatic transmissions only) and draw the MAF sensor signal.

_____ 5. What difference did you notice? _____

_____

DATE_____

INSTRUCTOR'S OK
_____

NAME_____

MAKE_____ MODEL_____ YR_____

SENSOR DIAGNOSIS USING DTCs WORKSHEET

Code diagnosis involves a step-by-step procedure to follow whenever there is a diagnostic trouble code (DTC) set in a vehicle computer.

_____ 1. Retrieve the diagnostic trouble code(s):

_____ _____ _____ _____

_____ 2. Perform a thorough visual inspection looking carefully for any obvious problems or evidence of previous repairs that could have caused the DTC(s) to set.

_____ 3. Check for any code-related technical service bulletins (TSBs).

_____ 4. Clear the DTC(s) and attempt to set the opposite code. For example, if the DTC is for an open sensor (high resistance), unplug the sensor and use a jumper wire to short the sensor terminals together (low resistance) opposite code set = _____.

    A. If the opposite code sets, the wiring is okay; the problem is a defective sensor.
    B. If the opposite code does not set, the wiring or the electrical connector is at fault.

    _____ The problem was a sensor.

    _____ The problem was the wiring or connector.

DATE_____

UNIT 9

COMPUTERIZED CARBURETOR DIAGNOSIS

NAME_____

_____

MAKE_____ MODEL_____ YR_____

CARBURETOR IDLE ADJUSTMENT WORKSHEET

The idle adjustment of a carburetor greatly affects the way the engine performs at idle and low speeds. The idle mixture screw adjustment also has a slight affect on the engine operation during cruise operation because the idle passages are still allowing some fuel flow even if most of the fuel is delivered through the main discharge nozzle.

_____ 1. Start and warm the engine to operating temperature. (The upper radiator hose is hot and pressurized until an electric cooling fan has cycled on and then off twice.)

_____ 2. Connect a tachometer to monitor the engine speed. Adjust idle speed until idle speed is close to specifications.

NOTE: This step is necessary to be assured that the throttle plate is adjusted correctly to allow the idle and low-speed carburetor circuit to be operating.

_____ 3. Adjust the idle mixture screw(s) either way until:

    A. the highest RPM reading.
    B. the highest engine vacuum (in inches of mercury).
    C. 50% duty cycle.
    D. 30° dwell.

_____ 4. After the idle mixture screws have been adjusted, readjust the idle speed to specifications.

    Idle speed specification = _____ RPM

DATE_____

_____

INSTRUCTOR'S OK

NAME_____

MAKE_____ MODEL_____ YR_____

M/C SOLENOID DWELL WORKSHEET
(General Motors CCC Carburetors Only)

_____ 1. Locate the dwell test connector (the blue wire with the green connector).

_____ 2. Connect the dwell meter (6-cylinder scale) to test the connector.

_____ 3. Start the engine.

_____ 4. Observe the dwell meter while in <u>open loop</u> at idle (should be fixed):

open loop dwell = _____.

_____ 5. Observe the dwell meter while in <u>closed loop</u> (should be varying):

dwell at 3,000 RPM = _____ (should be 25° to 45°).

dwell at idle RPM = _____ (should be 25° to 35°).

_____ 6. Create a large vacuum leak such as a PCV source hose. What does the dwell

meter indicate (it should decrease)? _____

_____

_____

_____ 7. Add some propane to the air intake. What does the dwell meter indicate

(it should increase)?_____

_____

_____

DATE_____

_____
INSTRUCTOR'S OK

NAME_____

MAKE_____ MODEL_____ YR_____

FLOAT LEVEL AND RESTRICTION TEST WORKSHEET
(General Motors carbureted vehicles)

On most General Motors carburetors, the float level can be measured externally by the use of a float gauge stick commonly called a "popsicle stick."

_____ 1. Select the properly calibrated float gauge stick for the carburetor being tested.

_____ 2. Float level reading = _____ in.   Float level specifications = _____ in.

Float level is **OK** _____   **NOT OK** _____

_____ 3. Start the engine and accelerate to about 2500 RPM.

_____ 4. Choke the engine by closing the choke and covering the carburetor with a shop cloth.

_____ 5. The float level should decrease when the engine dies, then rise quickly back to the original float level. If the float level does *not* return to its original reading or rises slowly, then the fuel filter, fuel line or fuel sock inside the fuel tank is restricted.

OK _____   **NOT OK** _____

DATE_____

INSTRUCTOR'S OK

NAME_____

MAKE_____ MODEL_____ YR_____

CARBURETOR SOLENOID DUTY CYCLE WORKSHEET

Most computer-controlled carburetors use a two-wire solenoid to control the air-fuel mixture. Most apply 12 volts to the solenoid and the computer grounds the solenoid with a varying duty cycle. Duty cycle is the percentage of time the solenoid is actuated.

The mixture supplied to the engine is rich when the solenoid is de-energized (0% duty cycle) and lean when the solenoid is energized all the time (100% duty cycle).

Mixture	Duty Cycle	Computer Command
Rich	90%	leaning the mixture
Lean	10%	richening the mixture
Ideal	50%	midrange of control

_____ 1. Connect the digital meter to the negative lead of the mixture control solenoid. Set the meter to read "duty cycle."

_____ 2. Start the engine and observe the duty cycle readings:

    A. The reading should be fixed while in open loop.
        reading = _____

    B. The reading should vary while in closed loop.
        reading range = _____ to _____

_____ 3. Disconnect a manifold vacuum hose. The duty cycle should decrease indicating that the computer is attempting to compensate for a lean mixture.

    OK _____ NOT OK _____

If not OK, check the oxygen sensor for proper operation. If the oxygen sensor is not functioning, then the computer cannot vary the duty cycle of the carburetor solenoid to keep the engine operating in fuel control.

DATE_____

INSTRUCTOR'S OK
_____

NAME_____

MAKE_____ MODEL_____ YR_____

SCOPE TESTING CARBURETOR MIXTURE-CONTROL SOLENOIDS WORKSHEET

A scope is an excellent tool for observing the operation of a computer-controlled carburetor mixture-control solenoid.

_____ 1. Connect the scope probe to the negative side of the mixture-control solenoid.

   HINT: On General Motors vehicles, the scope probe can be connected to the green M/C solenoid test lead.

_____ 2. Connect the scope probe ground lead to a clean metal component on the engine.

_____ 3. Set the scope settings as follows:

   Volts Per Division = 10 volts DC
   Time Per Division = 20 ms
   Trigger Level = 500 millivolts (0.5 V.)
   Trigger Slope = positive (+)

_____ 4. Start and run the engine and wait until it is operating at normal operating temperature in closed loop.

   A. What is the solenoid "on" time? _____ ms
   B. What is the voltage of the induction spike? _____ volts

   Draw the waveform here:

   ┌───┐
   │   │
   │   │
   │   │
   │   │
   │   │
   └───┘

   The scope pattern is: **OK** _____   **NOT OK** _____

DATE_____

UNIT 10

FUEL INJECTION TESTING AND SERVICE

INSTRUCTOR'S OK
_____

NAME_____

MAKE_____ MODEL_____ YR_____

FIELD SERVICE MODE WORKSHEET
(General Motors Fuel-injected Vehicles Only)

1. Turn the ignition key on (engine off).

2. The check engine light should be on.

3. Ground the terminal "B" of the ALCL and connect terminals A and B with jumper wire.

4. Check for any trouble codes = _____.

5. Start the engine and observe the "check engine" (service engine soon) light.

       blinking rapidly = open loop

       blinking slowly = closed loop

       if "on" longer than "off" = rich

       if "off" longer than "on" = lean

6. The estimated time in open loop = _____.

7. Is the mixture okay at idle? _____

8. Is the mixture okay at 2,000 RPM? _____

   NOTE: If possible, drive the vehicle. How does it perform?

_____

OK _____ **NOT OK** _____

DATE_____

NAME_____

INSTRUCTOR'S OK

MAKE_____ MODEL_____ YR_____

FUEL PUMP CURRENT DRAW TEST WORKSHEET

Many electric fuel pumps can be measured for current draw in amperes. A higher than normal amperage draw may indicate a clogged fuel filter causing back pressure for the pump or a worn pump.

GM Fuel-Injected Vehicles

NOTE: Other makes and models of vehicles can be tested by connecting the ammeter in series with the fuel pump fuse and then operating the engine. Check the wiring diagram for your specific vehicle.

Locate the fuel pump test lead. This test lead on General Motors vehicles may have a wire color of red, yellow, orange, gray, or tan with a black stripe. The plastic connector color is not important.

HINT: The color of the wire is the same on the fuel pump relay. This helps identify which relay is the fuel pump relay.

NOTE: On Pontiac Firebirds and Fieros and Chevrolet Camaros and Corvettes, the test terminal is located in terminal "G" (Lower left corner) of the ALCL (DLC).

Procedure:
- Connect the digital multimeter, set it to read amperes (A) and connect the red lead to the positive (+) of the battery. Connect the black lead to the fuel pump test terminal. The pump should run and an amperage reading should be observed on the meter.
  Confirm the reading with acceptable specifications.
  Reading = _____ amp(s)
  Normal readings: TBI = 3 to 5 amps (9-13 psi). Port injection = 4 to 6 amps (35-45 psi). Central port injection = 8 to 9 amps (55-64 psi).
- If the current is <u>lower</u> than specifications, check for:
  1. poor electrical connection at the fuel pump relay.
  2. poor connection at the fuel pump electrical connector.
  3. poor ground connection.
  4. leak between the pump and the tank outlet preventing proper buildup of pressure.
  NOTE: A very low fuel level can cause low current draw readings.
- If the current is <u>higher</u> than specifications, check for:
  1. clogged fuel filter.
  2. pinched fuel lines.
  3. slowly rotating fuel pump.

OK _____   NOT OK _____

DATE_____

_____
INSTRUCTOR'S OK

NAME_____

MAKE_____ MODEL_____ YR_____

FUEL PUMP TEST LIGHT WORKSHEET
(GM Fuel-injected Vehicles)

Locate the fuel pump test lead. This test lead on General Motors vehicles may have a wire color of red, yellow, orange, gray, or tan with a black stripe. The plastic connector color is not important.

HINT: The color of the wire is the same on the fuel pump relay. This helps identify which relay is the fuel pump relay.

NOTE: On Pontiac Firebirds and Fieros and Chevrolet Camaros and Corvettes, the test terminal is located in terminal "G" (lower left corner) of the ALCL (DLC).

Procedure:

_____ 1. Connect a standard 12-volt test light to the positive (+) terminal of the battery. Touch the test light probe end to the fuel pump test lead.

      NOTE: Test light may or may not be on at this step.

_____ 2. Turn the ignition switch to on (engine off). The test light should go out (or come on if originally on) for 2 seconds.

      OK ____   NOT OK ____

This test indicates that the computer is working. This is a fast and easy method to check that the computer has power and ground and is capable of supplying 12 volts to the relay. This 2-second on period is the time the computer turns on the fuel pump relay without a tach (RPM) signal. (If the computer receives a RPM signal, the fuel pump relay is obviously commanded to remain on.)

DATE _____

_____
INSTRUCTOR'S OK

NAME_____

MAKE_____ MODEL_____ YR_____

PORT FUEL-INJECTION SYSTEM DIAGNOSIS WORKSHEET

_____ 1. Attach a fuel pressure gauge to the Schrader valve on the fuel rail.

_____ 2. Turn the ignition key to "on" or start the engine to build up the fuel pump pressure.

  _____psi (should be about 35-45 psi)

_____ 3. Turn the ignition off and wait 20 minutes, and then observe the fuel pressure retained in the fuel rail = _____ psi.

(The fuel pressure should <u>not</u> drop more than 20 psi in 20 minutes.)

If the drop is less than 20 psi in 20 minutes, everything is OK.

If the drop is <u>greater</u> than 20 psi in 20 minutes, there is a possible problem with:
  A. the check valve in the fuel pump.
  B. leaking injectors.
  C. a defective (leaking) fuel pressure regulator.

To determine which unit is defective, perform the following:

Step #1:   Re-energize the electric fuel pump.
Step #2:   Clamp the fuel <u>supply</u> line, wait 10 minutes. If the pressure drop does <u>not</u> occur - replace the fuel pump. If the pressure drop still occurs - continue with Step #3.
Step #3:   Repeat the pressure buildup of the electric pump and clamp the fuel return line. If the pressure drop time is now OK, replace the fuel pressure regulator.
Step #4:   If the pressure drop still occurs, the injectors are leaking. Remove the injectors together with the fuel rail and hold over paper. Replace those injectors that drip a drop or more after 10 minutes with pressurized fuel.

CAUTION: Do not clamp plastic fuel lines. Connect shutoff valves to the fuel system to shut off supply and return lines.

  OK _____   **NOT OK** _____

DATE_____

INSTRUCTOR'S OK

NAME_____

MAKE_____ MODEL_____ YR_____

INJECTOR BALANCE TESTING WORKSHEET

(Ohmmeter Method/Voltage Drop)

_____ 1. Measure the resistance of all injectors with a digital ohmmeter. Use Kent-Moore

J-39021 to measure the voltage drop.

NOTE: For best performance and idle quality, all injectors should measure

within 0.3 to 0.4 ohms of each other. Injector resistances:

Resistance/Voltage Drop   Resistance/Voltage Drop

1. _____/_____   5. _____/_____

2. _____/_____   6. _____/_____

3. _____/_____   7. _____/_____

4. _____/_____   8. _____/_____

Highest resistance = ____ ohms.   Highest voltage drop = ____

Lowest resistance = ____ ohms.   Lowest voltage drop = ____

Difference   = ____ ohms.   Difference   = ____

OK_____ **NOT OK**_____   **OK**_____ **NOT OK**_____

DATE_____

NAME_____

MAKE_____ MODEL_____ YR_____

INJECTOR BALANCE TESTING WORKSHEET

(Pulse Unit Method)

1. Perform an injector balance test using a pulse unit.

    A. connect the fuel pressure gauge.

    B. energize the fuel pump to build pressure - note the reading.

    C. connect the pulse unit to the battery and injector-pulse unit and observe the pressure

    at the end of the pulse and record.

   Beginning Pressure   Pressure After Pulse

1. _____   _____
2. _____   _____
3. _____   _____
4. _____   _____
5. _____   _____
6. _____   _____
7. _____   _____
8. _____   _____

Highest drop _____

Lowest drop _____

Difference _____

(**NOTE**: All injectors should be within 1½ psi (10 kPa of each other.)

OK_____   NOT OK_____

DATE_____

NAME_____

INSTRUCTOR'S OK

MAKE_____ MODEL_____ YR_____

INJECTOR CLEANING WORKSHEET I

_____ 1. Disable the electric fuel pump:

   _____ A. fuse.

   _____ B. connector.

   _____ C. other.

_____ 2. Start the engine - allow it to die. Crank the engine an additional 10 seconds to reduce the rail pressure.

_____ 3. Remove the vacuum hose from the fuel pressure regulator and plug hose.

_____ 4. Connect the hose from the cleaning tank to the fuel pressure Schrader (service) valve connection.

   NOTE: Pressure in the cleaning tank should not exceed 25 psi to prevent the cleaning solution from returning to the fuel tank past the fuel pressure regulator.

_____ 5. Start and run the engine at a fast idle (2,000 RPM) for a maximum of 10 minutes.

_____ 6. Close the valve on the cleaner hose to run the engine out of fuel; crank the engine for 10 seconds to reduce pressure before removing the cleaning hose.

_____ 7. Reconnect the vacuum hose to the fuel pressure regulator and restore fuel pump operation.

DATE_____

NAME_____

_____
INSTRUCTOR'S OK

MAKE_____ MODEL_____ YR_____

INJECTOR CLEANING WORKSHEET II

_____ 1. Start the engine and run it until it reaches normal operating temperature.

_____ 2. Using a scan tool or frequency counter, record the O_2 cross counts at 1,000 RPM on #9 below.

_____ 3. Using the four-gas exhaust analyzer, record the exhaust gas information at idle (park) on #9 below.

_____ 4. Stop the engine and disable the fuel pump:

    A. remove the fuel pump fuse.

    *B. unplug the wiring to the fuel pump.   * Preferred method

_____ 5. Start the engine and allow it to stall. (This double checks that the fuel pump de-energization process was successful.)

_____ 6. Connect the injector cleaning equipment as demonstrated.

_____ 7. Operate the engine on the cleaning solution for a maximum of **ten minutes**; disconnect the cleaning equipment.

_____ 8. Reconnect the fuel pump.

_____ 9. Start the engine and record the O_2 cross counts and four-gas information:

Before	After	Change +/-
O_2 cross counts _____	O_2 cross counts _____	_____
HC............. _____	HC............. _____	_____
CO............. _____	CO............. _____	_____
CO_2............. _____	CO_2............. _____	_____
O_2............. _____	O_2............. _____	_____

DATE_____

INSTRUCTOR'S OK

NAME_____

MAKE_____ MODEL_____ YR_____

INJECTOR CLEANING WORKSHEET III

_____ 1. Before cleaning the injectors, make certain that all ignition components (coils, plug wires and spark plugs) are okay. Also check and clean deposits on the throttle plate(s).

_____ 2. Disable the electric fuel pump by disconnecting the wiring connector to the pump.

NOTE: On some vehicles, the fuel pump can be disabled by removing the fuel pump fuse.

_____ 3. Start the engine and allow it to stall. This tests that the fuel pump has been disabled.

_____ 4. Connect the hose from the cleaning tank to the fuel rail.

_____ 5. Pump up the cleaning tank to 20 psi.

_____ 6. Start the engine and run at a fast idle - do not permit the engine to stall.

_____ 7. Run the engine for a maximum of 10 minutes.

_____ 8. Close the valve on the cleaning tank hose and allow the engine to stall.

_____ 9. Remove the hose from the fuel rail Schrader valve and replace the cap.

_____10. Reconnect the fuel pump wiring connector or replace the fuel pump fuse.

_____11. Restart the engine and check for proper operation.

DATE_____

NAME_____

_____

MAKE_____ MODEL_____ YR_____

FUEL TRIM WORKSHEET

Fuel trim is the computer correction factor that uses the oxygen sensor to determine if more or less fuel needs to be delivered by the fuel injectors. Fuel trim is only available on a scan tool.

_____ 1. Connect a scan tool and select long-term fuel trim (LTFT) (block learn).

_____ 2. Start the engine and operate until normal operating temperature and closed loop status is achieved.

_____ 3. Record the following cell number and LTFT amount:

	Cell	LTFT
Idle in Drive (if automatic transmission only)	_____	_____
Idle in Park A/C off	_____	_____
Idle in Park A/C on	_____	_____
3000 RPM in Park	_____	_____

Results: Fuel trim should be within plus or minus 20% or within 118-138 if the block is displayed as a binary number.

OK _____ NOT OK _____

DATE_____

INSTRUCTOR'S OK
_____

NAME_____

MAKE_____ MODEL_____ YR_____

SCOPE TESTING A FUEL INJECTOR WORKSHEET

A scope is an excellent tool for observing the operation of a computer-controlled fuel injector.

_____ 1. Locate the fuel injector to be tested and use a T-pin to back probe the negative (ground) lead at the injector.

> **HINT:** An easy way to determine which lead is the power side and which lead is the ground side of the injector connector is to simply unplug the connector at the injector. Turn the ignition switch on (engine off). Use a voltmeter to determine which terminal has voltage; this terminal is the power side of the injector. You want to T-pin the other (ground side) terminal.

_____ 2. Connect the scope probe to the T-pin and connect the probe ground lead to a clean non-painted engine component.

_____ 3. Set the scope settings as follows:

> Volts per division = 10 volts DC
> Time per division = 1 millisecond (1 ms) (adjust as necessary to display one
>   complete injector pulse on the display)
> Trigger level = 500 millivolts (0.5 V)
> Trigger slope = negative (-)
> Trigger delay = -2 divisions

_____ 4. Start the engine and allow it to idle and observe the waveform.
   A. What is the injector "on" time? _____ ms
   B. What is the peak voltage of the inductive "kick" that occurred when the injector was turned off? _____ volts

   Draw the waveform here:

_____ 5. Increase the engine speed to 2000 RPM.

   A. What is the injection "on" time? _____ms
   B. What is the peak voltage of the inductive kick that occurred when the injector was turned off? _____ volts

   Scope pattern is   **OK** _____   **NOT OK** _____

                                      DATE_____

NAME_____

MAKE_____ MODEL_____ YR_____

INJECTOR GROUND TESTING WORKSHEET

The vehicle computer provides the ground for the injector to complete the electrical circuit. When the computer removes the ground, the injector shuts off and stops delivering fuel. When the injector is being turned on, the voltage at the ground terminal of the injector should be close to zero.

_____ 1. Connect a digital multimeter to the ground terminal of an injector using a T-pin or back probe tool.

> **CAUTION:** DO NOT pierce the wiring insulation.

_____ 2. Set the digital meter to DC volts.

_____ 3. Start and operate the engine at idle speed.

_____ 4. Set the meter to MIN/MAX record (use one millisecond (1 ms) setting for best results).

_____ 5. Touch MIN/MAX to observe the lowest reading

lowest voltage = _____ volts (should be less than 0.6 V) (600 millivolts)

If the voltage is greater than 1 V (1000 mV), then the problem could be:

A. poor computer ground - perform a computer ground voltage drop test.

B. faulty injector drive transistor - if the computer ground voltage drop is okay and an injector problem still exists, the computer itself needs to be replaced if the injector voltage does not approach 0 volts while being energized.

OK _____   NOT OK _____

DATE _____

_____
INSTRUCTOR'S OK

NAME_____

MAKE_____ MODEL_____ YR_____

GM 2.8/3.1-LITER V-6 INJECTOR WORKSHEET

General Motors has equipped many different vehicles with the 2.8/3.1-liter 60° V-6. From 1985 until 1996, this port-injected engine used a computer that pulsed three injectors at a time (multiport instead of sequential). An electrical fault in one fuel injector can be easily detected using an ohmmeter without having to remove the intake manifold plenum to gain access to the injectors individually. Three injectors wound in parallel should read 1/3 of the resistance of each injector.

_____ 1. Locate the electrical connector that connects the injector (or engine) harness to the vehicle body wiring harness. Two places are commonly used:

A. the connector attached to the rear of the intake manifold.

B. the connector located near the computer on the right inside front fender.

_____ 2. Check with the service manual for the two pairs of wires used to provide a power (+) and a ground (-) to the two injector groups of three.

Color of the positive (power) wires = _____

Color of the ground (computer-controlled) wires = _____

_____ 3. Use the digital multimeter set to read ohms.

_____ 4. Measure each group of three injectors: Group #1 = _____ ohms.

Group #2 = _____ ohms.

_____ 5. Both groups should be equal and within 0.3 ohm. **OK** _____ **NOT OK** _____

If the resistance of the grouped injectors is not within 0.3 ohm, then the intake manifold has to be removed to test each individual injector.

DATE _____

UNIT 11

EMISSION CONTROL DEVICE DIAGNOSIS

INSTRUCTOR'S OK

NAME_____

MAKE_____ MODEL_____ YR____

PCV SYSTEM TEST WORKSHEET

The purpose of the "positive crankcase ventilation" (PCV) system is to use engine intake manifold vacuum to draw crankcase vapors into the engine to be burned. These vapors occur due to blowby past the piston rings into the crankcase.

NOTE: If there is gasoline in the engine oil, gasoline vapors will be drawn into the engine and the intake charge will be richer. Therefore, if black exhaust smoke or a rich condition is being diagnosed, check the crankcase for the presence of gasoline.

A good PCV system should draw fresh air into the engine through a filter usually located in the air cleaner or on the valve (cam) cover. This filtered air then is mixed with the blowby gases in the crankcase and through a PCV valve which regulates the flow into the engine.

PCV Valve Operation:

A. idle = high vacuum = PCV valve almost closed by high vacuum.

B. at cruise = 10-15 in. Hg = PCV valve is opened to allow the crankcase gases to be drawn into the engine (vacuum and internal spring are almost balanced).

C. at wide open throttle (W.O.T.) low vacuum = PCV valve is fully opened by internal spring permitting maximum flow.

Testing the System:

_____ 1. Start the engine and allow it to idle.

_____ 2. Remove the oil fill cap.

_____ 3. Place a piece of paper or a 3" × 5" card over the filler. (The PCV system is functioning correctly if the paper is held down tight onto the filler by vacuum in the crankcase).

_____ 4. Seal off the oil fill opening and measure the crankcase vacuum at the dipstick tube = _____ (should be about 0.5 in. Hg or 7 in. of water if using a water manometer).

OK _____ NOT OK _____

DATE_____

_____
INSTRUCTOR'S OK

MAKE_____ MODEL_____ YR_____

AIR PUMP WORKSHEET

AIR means "air injection reaction." An AIR pump supplies additional air to the exhaust system to reduce carbon monoxide (CO) and unburned gasoline (hydrocarbons or HC) exhaust emissions. Most AIR pump systems supply air to the exhaust manifold (exhaust ports) until the engine reaches closed loop operation. As soon as the computer reaches closed loop, the air flow is directed to the catalytic converter to help the catalyst oxidize the HC and CO into harmless water (H_2O) and carbon dioxide (CO_2).

_____ 1. Locate the air pump.

_____ 2. Carefully inspect the condition of all of the hoses, check the valves and the metal lines for corrosion or damage.

_____ 3. Start the engine and feel the air pump lines to confirm the proper air flow.

> **NOTE:** A defective one-way check valve at the exhaust manifold can allow hot exhaust gases to flow past the check valve and cause damage to the switching valves, hoses or air pump itself. These exhaust gases can cause poor engine operation and stalling if drawn into the air intake system.

_____ 4. Inspect the air pump drive belt for cracks and proper tension.

   OK _____ NOT OK _____

DATE_____

NAME_____

MAKE_____ MODEL_____ YR_____

CANISTER PURGE WORKSHEET

Since the early 1970s, vehicles have been equipped with a charcoal (carbon) canister used to attract and hold gasoline vapors. Because carbon attracts carbon, the charcoal in the canister attracts the gasoline (hydrocarbon) vapors that would normally be lost to the atmosphere. Unburned hydrocarbon contributes to photochemical smog.

_____ 1. Locate the charcoal canister.

_____ 2. Using a hand-operated vacuum pump, check that all vacuum diaphragms that control the flow from the canister to the intake manifold can hold vacuum..

OK _____   **NOT OK** _____

_____ 3. Connect a canister purge flow gauge between the canister and the intake manifold. A good canister purge system should flow at least one liter per minute.

Amount of canister purge = _____ liter per minute.

NOTE: Sometimes this test cannot be performed without driving the vehicle. Some computer-controlled charcoal canister systems require that the vehicle be above a certain speed before the canister is purged.

OK _____   **NOT OK** _____

DATE_____

_____
INSTRUCTOR'S OK

EGR VALVE DIAGNOSIS WORKSHEET

The purpose and function of the exhaust gas recirculation (EGR) valve is to blend a slight amount (about 7%) of exhaust gas into the fresh intake charge entering the combustion chamber. The burned exhaust gases are inert and therefore, cannot react chemically with the burning process. The exhaust gases take up mass in the combustion chamber and slow the burning of the air/fuel mixture reducing the peak temperatures that would normally occur if the exhaust gases were not present. This prevents combustion chamber temperatures from exceeding 2500° F (1370° C) and reduces the formation of oxides of nitrogen (NOx) exhaust emissions.

A typical EGR problem:

• Too much EGR flow causes rough idle and stalling (engine could operate okay at highway speeds).

• Too little EGR flow causes spark knock (ping or detonation) and excessive NOx emissions especially during cruise and moderate acceleration.

_____ 1. Locate the EGR valve.

_____ 2. Start and operate the engine to 2000 RPM and apply vacuum to the EGR valve. A noticeable drop in engine performance should be noticed.

> **NOTE:** Some EGR valves use computer-controlled solenoids. Most electronically-controlled solenoid type EGR systems can be tested using a scan tool.

OK _____   **NOT OK** _____

DATE_____

_____   NAME_____
INSTRUCTOR'S OK

MAKE_____ MODEL_____ YR_____

CATALYTIC CONVERTER TEST WORKSHEET
(Temperature Difference Method)

A catalytic converter uses a catalyst to start a chemical reaction, but does not enter into the chemical reaction. Because a chemical reaction causes heat, the temperature of the catalytic converter should be at least 10% hotter at the outlet as compared to the temperature of the inlet.

_____ 1. Start the engine and run at a fast idle (2,500 RPM) for at least 2 minutes to fully warm up the oxygen sensor, the engine coolant, and the catalytic converter.

_____ 2. Using a pyrometer (infrared or contact type), measure the front (inlet) and outlet of the catalytic converter.

        Inlet temperature   = _____°

        Outlet temperature = _____°

        Difference   = _____°

_____ 3. Results: If the outlet temperature is 50°F (10°C) (or 10%) higher than the inlet temperature, the catalytic converter is functioning correctly.

        OK _____   **NOT OK** _____

NOTE: Some engines operate so cleanly that the catalytic converter has limited emissions to convert and, therefore, the temperature of the converter may not show an increase in temperature. To check if the catalytic converter is functioning on a vehicle with very low exhaust emissions, simply use a vacuum hose connected to a spark plug wire and temporarily ground out one cylinder by using a tester light or jumper wire attached to ground. Measure the inlet and outlet temperatures of the converter while one cylinder is grounded out. To avoid damage to the catalytic converter, do not ground out a cylinder for longer than 10 seconds.

DATE_____

NAME_____

INSTRUCTOR'S OK

MAKE_____ MODEL_____ YR_____

CATALYTIC CONVERTER TEST WORKSHEET

(Rattle Test)

_____ 1. Safely hoist the vehicle.

_____ 2. Using your fist or a small rubber mallet, lightly tap on the catalytic converter. If the converter rattles, it is broken internally and requires replacement.

OK _____ NOT OK _____

DATE_____

_____
INSTRUCTOR'S OK

NAME_____

MAKE_____ MODEL_____ YR_____

EXHAUST BACK PRESSURE TEST WORKSHEET

A clogged or partially restricted exhaust greatly affects engine performance. Lack of power is a common symptom of a partially restricted exhaust system. In severe cases, the engine may start/stall due to exhaust system restriction.

_____ 1. Remove the oxygen sensor from the exhaust manifold and install tool to measure exhaust back pressure.

> **NOTE:** This tool can be made from an old oxygen sensor and a short piece of pipe such as a brake line. Simply knock out the center of the oxygen sensor and braze or epoxy the tube to the sensor housing.

_____ 2. Connect a vacuum/pressure gauge to the exhaust back pressure tool. Start the engine and run at idle and observe exhaust back pressure.

> _____ psi back pressure (maximum allowable back pressure at idle is 1.25 psi.)

> **OK** _____ **NOT OK** _____

_____ 3. Operate the engine at a constant speed of 2500 RPM and observe the exhaust back pressure.

> _____ psi back pressure (Maximum allowable back pressure at 2500 RPM is 2.5 psi.)

> **OK** _____ **NOT OK** _____

DATE_____

UNIT 12

5-GAS EXHAUST ANALYSIS

NAME_____

INSTRUCTOR'S OK

NAME_____

MAKE_____ MODEL_____ YR_____

5-GAS EXHAUST ANALYSIS WORKSHEET

	No Catalytic Converter	With Catalytic Converter
HC -	300 PPM or less	30 - 50 PPM or less
CO -	3% or less	0.3 - 0.5% or less
CO_2 -	12% - 15%	12% - 15%
O_2 -	1% - 2%	1% - 2%
NOx -	less than 1000 PPM	less than 1000 PPM

high HC = ignition problem (or excessively lean [lean misfire]).

high CO = fuel system problem (lack of air).

O_2 = the higher, the leaner (vacuum leak, clogged injector, etc.).

_____ 1. Record all four gases @ idle:

HC _____ CO_2 _____

CO _____ O_2 _____   NOx_____

The idle test results indicate what possible problem?

_____

_____ 2. Record all four gases @ 2,500 RPM:

HC _____ CO_2 _____

CO _____ O_2 _____   NOx_____

The cruise RPM test indicates what possible problem?

_____

DATE_____

NAME_____

MAKE_____ MODEL_____ YR____

CYLINDER DE-CARBONIZING WORKSHEET

_____ 1. Run the engine until normal operating temperature and record exhaust gas readings. Exhaust readings before de-carbonizing the engine:

	IDLE	2000 RPM
HC =	_____	_____
CO =	_____	_____
CO_2 =	_____	_____
O_2 =	_____	_____
NOx =	_____	_____

_____ 2. A. Connect the carbon cleaning machine according to the manufacturer's recommendation.

OR

B. Mix a can of top engine cleaner (such as General Motors Top Engine Cleaner #1050002) with another can of water into a large coffee can. Use 5/32" vacuum hose connected to the manifold vacuum and draw mixture into the engine while maintaining at least 1000 RPM.

_____ 3. Drive vehicle aggressively until all exhaust smoke disappears. Retest the exhaust gasses.

	IDLE	2000 RPM
HC =	_____	_____
CO =	_____	_____
CO_2 =	_____	_____
O_2 =	_____	_____
NOx =	_____	_____

DATE_____

INSTRUCTOR'S OK _____

NAME_____

MAKE_____ MODEL_____ YR____

ENGINE FUEL CONTROL TESTING WORKSHEET

_____ 1. Determine any stored trouble codes:

_____ _____
_____ _____
_____ _____

Are the codes stored "hard" (current problems) or "soft" (history problems) codes?

_____

_____ 2. Back probe the oxygen sensor signal wire at the connector using a T-pin. Using a digital high-impedance meter, measure the oxygen sensor voltage (should fluctuate between 200 - 800 mV.).

Results: _____
Was the oxygen sensor voltage varying? **YES** _____ **NO** _____

(The computer is operating in closed loop if the oxygen voltage is varying above and below 500 mV.)

Is the computer operating in closed loop? **YES** _____ **NO** _____

_____ 3. Disconnect a large vacuum hose such as the hose leading to the brake vacuum boosters while observing the voltmeter. Did the oxygen sensor voltage drop when the leak was introduced? **YES** _____ **NO** _____

_____ 4. Add propane to the air inlet of the engine while observing the voltmeter connected to the oxygen sensor. Did the oxygen sensor voltage rise when the propane was added? **YES** _____ **NO** _____

_____ 5. If the oxygen sensor responded to both the vacuum leak and the propane, the computer is capable of correcting the fuel mixture based on oxygen sensor (O2S) input. Therefore the engine is said to be in fuel control.

_____ 6. If the O2S can respond to both a vacuum leak and the addition of propane, then the engine is operating in fuel control.

_____ 7. Is the engine operating in fuel control? **YES** _____ **NO** _____

DATE_____

UNIT 13

ENGINE CONDITION DIAGNOSIS

_____
INSTRUCTOR'S OK

RELATIVE COMPRESSION WORKSHEET

Many scopes such as the Fluke 98 scopemeter and Bear ACE are capable of displaying changes in battery voltage when the engine is being cranked and display a relative compression based on the voltage change. For example, if a particular cylinder is weak and lacks compression, the starter motor will not have to draw as much current from the battery whenever that cylinder is being rotated through its compression stroke. The lower compression is reflected by a higher than normal battery voltage and displayed on the display as a lower than normal reading.

_____ 1. Connect the scope to the battery positive (+) and negative (-) terminals. Connect a probe to cylinder #1 needed to "sync" the display to cylinder #1. (Check and follow the scope manufacturer's recommended procedure.)

_____ 2. Disable the ignition to prevent the engine from starting while it is being cranked.

     A. On vehicles equipped with a distributor and separate coil, unplug the coil wire from the distributor cap and <u>ground</u> the coil wire to a good engine ground using a jumper wire.
     B. Unplug the power lead feeding the ignition system (the white connector or side of General Motors HEI integral coil distributor).
     C. Unplug the wiring connector at the ignition coil

     NOTE: The ignition system must be disabled or grounded to prevent possible ignition coil damage that could result.

_____ 3. Crank the engine for 15 seconds and observe the scope pattern. If all cylinders are almost equal condition, the display should also be equal. If unequal test results are indicated, the engine should be tested further by performing a compression test and a cylinder leakage test.

     OK _____ NOT OK _____

DATE_____

NAME_____

_____
INSTRUCTOR'S OK

MAKE_____ MODEL_____ YR_____

POWER BALANCE WORKSHEET

_____ 1. Install 2" long vacuum hose between the distributor cap (or coils) and the spark plug wires.

_____ 2. Connect the tachometer to the engine and record idle RPM = _____.

_____ 3. Disconnect the O_2 sensor and the idle speed control to prevent the computer from compensating engine speed.

_____ 4. Using a test light, ground out one cylinder at a time by touching the tip of the grounded test light to the section of rubber hose, and record the RPM drop:

   #1 _____   #5 _____

   #2 _____   #6 _____

   #3 _____   #7 _____

   #4 _____   #8 _____

   NOTE: 50 RPM is the maximum variation between cylinders.
   The cylinder whose RPM drops the most is
   the <u>strongest</u> cylinder. The cylinder whose
   RPM drops the least is the <u>weakest</u> cylinder.

_____ 5. Results:

   RPM difference between the strongest and weakest cylinder _____.

   Which cylinder is the strongest? _____.

   Which cylinder is the weakest? _____.

   OK_____   **NOT OK_____**

                              DATE_____

NAME_____

INSTRUCTOR'S OK

MAKE_____ MODEL_____ YR_____

COMPRESSION TESTING WORKSHEET

_____ 1. Remove all spark plugs (be certain to label the spark plug wires).

_____ 2. Block open the throttle and choke (if equipped).

_____ 3. Perform compression testing during cranking (4 "puffs").

   NOTE: For accurate test results, the engine should be at normal operating temperature. The first puff should be at least 50% of the final puff. (A low first puff reading indicates possible weak piston rings.)

   RESULTS: First puff/final reading   First puff/final reading

   1. _____/_____   5. _____/_____
   2. _____/_____   6. _____/_____
   3. _____/_____   7. _____/_____
   4. _____/_____   8. _____/_____

4. Reinstall all spark plugs except one. Perform a running compression test at idle and at 2,000 RPM for each cylinder. Running compression should be equal among all cylinders. (Variations would indicate valve train related problems.)

   Idle   2,000 RPM

   1. _____   1. _____
   2. _____   2. _____
   3. _____   3. _____
   4. _____   4. _____
   5. _____   5. _____
   6. _____   6. _____
   7. _____   7. _____
   8. _____   8. _____

   OK _____   **NOT OK** _____

   DATE_____

NAME_____

_____
INSTRUCTOR'S OK

MAKE_____ MODEL_____ YR_____

CYLINDER LEAKAGE TEST WORKSHEET

_____ 1. The engine should be at normal operating temperature.

_____ 2. Test the cylinder with the piston at top dead center (TDC) on the compression stroke.

_____ 3. Calibrate the meter.

_____ 4. Install compressed air in the cylinder. Read the meter.

      _____ % of Leakage

      Check one:

      _____ Good   - less than 10%

      _____ Acceptable   - less than 20%

      _____ Unacceptable - higher than 20%

_____ 5. Check the <u>source</u> of air leakage:

      _____ A. radiator - possible blown head gasket or cracked cylinder head.

      _____ B. tail pipe - defective exhaust valve(s).

      _____ C. carburetor or air inlet - defective intake valve(s).

      _____ D. oil fill cap - possible worn or defective piston rings.

      OK _____   **NOT OK** _____

DATE_____

INSTRUCTOR'S OK

TIMING CHAIN DIAGNOSIS WORKSHEET

A worn or stretched timing chain causes the engine to lack power at lower speeds, yet perform okay at higher speeds.

_____ 1. Disable the ignition system.

_____ 2. Rotate the engine to TDC on the timing mark in normal direction of engine rotation (clockwise as viewed from the front of the engine).

_____ 3. Remove the distributor cap.

_____ 4. Rotate the engine counterclockwise as viewed from the front of the engine (non-principle end) until the rotor just starts to move.

> **NOTE:** On engines equipped with distributorless ignition, observe the movement of the valve train rather than the distributor rotor.

_____ 5. Record the number of degrees of slack in the timing chain.

_____ number of degrees of slack

OK_____   NOT OK_____

Results:

1. less than 5° = normal.

2. 5° - 8° = some change in engine operation if the timing chain is replaced.

3. over 8° = new timing chain definitely required.

DATE_____

_____
INSTRUCTOR'S OK

VACUUM TESTING WORKSHEET

_____ 1. Connect the vacuum gauge to a manifold vacuum source.

_____ 2. Vacuum at idle = _____ in. Hg (should be 17-21 in. Hg and steady)

_____ 3. Drive the vehicle on a level road in high gear at a steady speed.

  Cruise vacuum = _____ in. Hg (should be 10 - 15 in. Hg)

_____ 4. Accelerate the vehicle in high gear to W.O.T.

  W.O.T. vacuum = _____ in. Hg (should be almost zero)

_____ 5. Decelerate the vehicle from 50 MPH with the throttle closed.

  Deceleration vacuum = _____ in. Hg (should be higher than idle vacuum)

_____ 6. With the engine out of gear and the brake firmly applied, raise the engine speed to 2,000 RPM and hold for one full minute. This tests for an exhaust restriction.

  Results = _____ in. Hg

_____ 7. Stop the engine. Disable the ignition. Crank the engine and observe the vacuum during cranking.

  Cranking vacuum = _____ in. Hg (should be higher than 2.5 in. Hg)

  OK_____   NOT OK_____

DATE_____

INSTRUCTOR'S OK

NAME_____

MAKE_____ MODEL_____ YR____

ATF TEST WORKSHEET

Perform this procedure whenever sticking valve guides are suspected. A rough idle with a low and unstable vacuum reading is a usual symptom.

_____ 1. Operate the engine until it reaches normal operating temperature (upper radiator hose hot and pressurized or until the cooling fan cycles on and off twice).

_____ 2. Connect the vacuum gauge and record the vacuum at idle:

_____.

_____ 3. Add about 4 ounces of ATF into the air inlet:

    A.   <u>Carburetor or TBI</u> - Raise engine speed to a fast idle (about 2,000 RPM) and hold. Pour ATF down the carburetor as fast as possible and do not allow the engine to stall.

    B.   <u>Port Fuel Injection</u> - Secure a vacuum hose about 2 feet long and connect it to a vacuum port. With the engine at a fast idle, place the hose into a container of ATF. The engine vacuum will draw the ATF from the container into the engine.

_____ 4. Run the engine several minutes until the engine stops smoking. Record the vacuum at idle _____.

_____ 5. Describe the results: _____

_____

DATE_____

NAME_____

INSTRUCTOR'S OK

MAKE_____ MODEL_____ YR_____

OIL PRESSURE MEASUREMENT WORKSHEET

_____ 1. Locate the oil pressure sending (sender) unit.

_____ 2. Remove the sending unit.

_____ 3. Thread the mechanical oil pressure gauge into the threaded portion of the engine block where the sending unit was located.

_____ 4. Route the oil pressure gauge hose away from the moving components of the engine.

_____ 5. Start the engine and check for leaks.

_____ 6. Record the oil pressure:

      oil pressure @ idle _____

      oil pressure @ 1,000 RPM _____

      oil pressure @ 2,000 RPM _____

      oil pressure @ 3,000 RPM _____

      NOTE: Most engines require about 10 psi per 1,000 RPM.

_____ 7. Results: (check one)

      great _____ (over 10 psi per 1,000 RPM)

      good _____ (at 10 psi per 1,000 RPM)

      bad _____ (less than 10 psi per 1,000 RPM)

DATE_____

NAME_____

INSTRUCTOR'S OK
_____

MAKE_____ MODEL_____ YR_____

VOLTMETER CHECK OF ENGINE COOLANT WORKSHEET

_____ 1. Set the voltmeter to read on a low DC volt scale.

_____ 2. With the engine cool, carefully remove the radiator cap.

_____ 3. Place one voltmeter lead into the coolant and the other lead to ground (the neck of the radiator if a brass radiator) or to a good body or engine ground.

   NOTE: The best "ground" is always the negative (-) terminal of the battery.

_____ 4. Results: _____ volt

   0.2 volt or less is acceptable.

   0.5 is borderline.

   0.7 volt or higher is unacceptable.

   (coolant should be replaced after flushing)

   IMPORTANT NOTE: If the voltmeter shows a high reading with relatively new coolant (antifreeze), it could be the result of a blown head gasket. A blown head gasket would allow combustion gases to enter the cooling system. When these gases combine with water, they form acids. It is the acid that causes the chemical reaction that produces the voltage in the coolant.

   OK_____   **NOT OK**_____

DATE_____

NAME_____

INSTRUCTOR'S OK

MAKE_____ MODEL_____ YR_____

ENGINE COOLANT TEMPERATURE WORKSHEET

For best engine performance, maximum fuel economy, and lowest possible exhaust emissions, the temperature of the engine coolant should be correct. Compare the normal operating coolant temperature to the thermostat rating.

THERMOSTAT RATING	OPENING TEMPERATURE	TEMPERATURE FULLY OPEN	ENGINE OPERATING TEMPERATURE RANGE
180°F (82°C)	180°F (82°C)	200°F (93°C)	180-200°F (82-93°C)
195°F (91°C)	195°F (91°C)	215°F (102°C)	195-215°F (91-102°C)

_____ 1. Start the engine and operate it until normal operating temperature is achieved (upper radiator hose is pressurized or the coolant fan cycles on and off twice).

_____ 2. Measure the temperature of the coolant near the thermostat housing using an infrared or contact-type pyrometer.

Temperature at thermostat housing = _____.

_____ 3. Observe the vehicle's dash temperature gauge and record where the temperature is indicated = _____.

_____ 4. Connect a scan tool and record the engine coolant temperature (ECT) value. ECT value = _____.

_____ 5. Do all the temperature readings agree?   **YES** ___   **NO** ___

_____ 6. Is the thermostat working correctly?   **YES** ___   **NO** ___

DATE_____

UNIT 14

SYMPTOM-BASED DIAGNOSIS

NAME_____

INSTRUCTOR'S OK

MAKE_____ MODEL_____ YR_____

NO-CODE DIAGNOSIS WORKSHEET

No-code diagnosis involves a step-by-step procedure to follow in the diagnosis of a problem when there are no stored diagnostic trouble codes (DTCs).

_____ 1. Verify the problem (concern).

_____ 2. Perform a thorough visual inspection.

_____ 3. Check for any technical service bulletins (TSBs).

_____ 4. If scan data is available, check the following:

      A. ECT and IAT are reasonable.
      B. IAC counts are within 15 to 25 counts.
      C. Oxygen sensor voltage transition is from below 200 mV to above 800 mV.
      D. Check long-term fuel trim (LTFT). It should be within + or - 10%.
      E. Check TP sensor for proper operation.

_____ 5. If scan data is _not_ available, check the oxygen sensor and TP sensor using a digital multimeter or scope.

      A. Oxygen sensor voltage should transition rapidly below 200 mV and above 800 mV.
      B. Throttle position (TP) sensor voltage should be either the specification at idle and transition to wide open throttle without a fault.

_____ 6. Remove a vacuum hose and observe the O2S voltage (it should go down, then start fluctuating again between 200 and 800 mV).

_____ 7. Add a small amount of propane to the air intake with the engine running at idle speed and observe the O2S voltage (it should go up, then start fluctuating again between 200 and 800 mV).

      OK _____ **NOT OK** _____

_____ 8. Is the engine operation in fuel control?　**YES** _____ **NO** _____

DATE_____

_____ PERSON DOING THE BUGGING _____

INSTRUCTOR'S OK

PERSON DOING THE DE-BUGGING _____

MAKE _____ MODEL _____ YEAR _____

PRACTICE BUG WORKSHEET

Rules for Fault Installation
- All faults must be "real world".
- The customer's concern must be stated.
- You must be able to explain what the fault will do and verify it.
- Do not damage wires or components.

_____ 1. State the customer's concern as it would be normally written on the repair order (RO).

_____

_____

_____ 2. Procedure (list troubleshooting actions step by step):

A. _____   F. _____
B. _____   G. _____
C. _____   H. _____
D. _____   I. _____
E. _____   J. _____

_____ 3. Time needed to find and correct the "bug" = _____.

_____ 4. Conclusion: _____

_____ 5. Results (check one):

A. correct   _____
B. almost correct   _____
C. close, but no cigar _____
D. incorrect   _____

DATE_____

APPENDIX

DATA STREAM VALUES

Scan tool values should be observed when all of the following conditions are met:

Engine @ Idle	**Upper Radiator Hose Hot**	**Closed Loop**
Accessories Off	**Park or Neutral**	**Closed Throttle**

PARAMETER	UNITS DISPLAYED	TYPICAL DATA VALUE
Desired RPM	RPM	ECM idle command (varies with temp)
RPM	RPM	± 100 RPM from desired RPM (± 50 in drive)
ECT	C°	85 to 108 degrees (185 to 226° F)
IAT	C°	10 to 80 degrees (50 to 176°F) (depends on underhood temp)
MAP	Volts	1 to 2 (usually 1.0 to 1.6)
BARO	Volts	2.5 to 5.5 (depends on altitude and baro pressure) (usually 4.6 to 4.8)
MAF	Gm/Sec	3 to 7
O2S	Volts	100 to 1000 mV
TP Sensor	Volts	0.45 to 0.65
Throttle Angle	0 to 100%	0%
IAC	Counts (steps)	5 to 50 (16 to 20 preferred)
Injector Pulse Width	Milliseconds	0.8 to 3.5 (usually 1.5 to 3.5)
P/N Switch	P/N and RDL	Park/Neutral (P/N)
STFT	Counts	-20% to +20%
LTFT	Counts	-20% to +20%
Open/Closed Loop	Open/Closed	Closed Loop (may go open with extended idle 0 or 1 - depends on air flow and RPM
VSS	MPH	0
TCC	On/Off	Off/(On with TCC command)
EGR Duty Cycle	0 to 100%	0 at idle
Spark Advance	# of Degrees	Varies
Knock Retard	Retard Degrees	0
Knock Signal	Yes/No	No
Battery	Volts	13.5 to 15.0
Fan	On/Off	Off (below 106°C)
P/S Switch	Norm/Hi Press	Normal
A/C Request	Yes/No	No (Yes with A.C requested)
A/C Clutch	On/Off	Off (on with A/C commanded on)
Fan Request	Yes/No	No (Yes, with A/C high pressure

13	O_2 sensor circuit		59	Transmission fluid temperature (low temperature)
14	ECT - high temperature		65	Fuel injector (low current)
15	ECT - low temperature		66	A/C refrigerant pressure sensor circuit (low)/or 3-2 shift control
16	Low voltage		67	CC solenoid circuit fault
17	Camshaft sensor circuit		68	Transmission slipping
21	TP sensor (voltage high)		69	CC stuck on
22	TP sensor (voltage low)		70	A/C refrigerant pressure sensor circuit (high)
23	IAT sensor (low temperature)		72	Loss of transmission output speed signal
24	VS sensor		73	Transmission pressure control solenoid circuit
25	IAT sensor (high temperature)		74	Transmission Input Speed (TIS) Sensor Circuit
26	QUAD - driver module circuit (MIL and gauges)		75	Digital EGR #1 error/or system voltage low
27	QUAD - driver module circuit (EVAP SOL and TCC)		76	Digital EGR #2 error
28	Transmission range (TR) pressure switch assembly (4L80-E); or QUAD - driver module circuit (A/C clutch relays)		77	Digital EGR #3 error
			79	VSS (high)/or transmission fluid over temperature
29	QUAD - driver module circuit for 4T60		80	VSS (low)
33	MAP sensor circuit (low vacuum)		81	Brake switch error/or 2-3 shift solenoid circuit
34	MAP sensor circuit (high vacuum)		82	Ignition control 3 X signal error/or 1-2 shift solenoid circuit
35	IAC - idle speed error		83	TCC PWM solenoid circuit fault
36	24 X signal circuit error (3.4 SFI)		85	PROM error/or transmission ratio error
37	Brake switch stuck on		86	Transmission low ratio error
38	Brake switch stuck off		87	A/D error/or transmission high ratio error
39	TCC stuck off		87	EEPROM error
42	Ignition control circuit error			
43	Knock sensor (KS) circuit			
44	O_2 - lean exhaust			
45	O_2 - rich exhaust			
51	EPROM error			
52	System voltage high			
53	Battery over voltage			
54	Low voltage to fuel pump			
55	Power enrichment too lean			
58	Transmission fluid temperature (high temperature)			

TYPICAL FORD DIAGNOSTIC TROUBLE CODES

11	Pass
12	RPM not within self-test upper RPM limit band
13	RPM not within self-test lower RPM limit band
13	DC motor did not move (2.3/2.5/1.0L CFI)
13	DC motor does not follow dashpot (2.3/2/5/1.01L CFI)
14	PIP circuit fault
15	ROM test failed
16	RPM too low to perform fuel test
18	Loss of tach input to processor - SPOUT circuit grounded
19	Failure in EEC reference voltage
21	Indicates ECT out of self-test range
22	Indicates MAP/BP out of self-test range
23	Indicates TP out of self-test range
24	Indicates ACT out of self-test range
25	Knock not sensed during dynamic response test
29	Insufficient input from VSS
31	EPT/EVP below minimum voltage
32	EVP voltage out of static limit
32	EGR valve not seated (PFE)
33	EGR valve not opening
34	Insufficient EGR flow (1.9L, 2.3L T/C EFI/2.3L, 3.8L CFI)
34	EVP voltage above static limit (SONIC)
34	Defective EPT sensor (PFE)
34	Exhaust pressure high/defective EPT sensor
35	EPT/EVP circuit above maximum voltage
41	EGO sensor circuit indicates system lean, no EGO switch detected
42	EGO sensor circuit indicates system rich, no EGO switch detected
43	EGO lean at WOI
44	Thermactor air system inoperative (cylinders 1-4 dual EGO)
45	Thermactor air upstream during self-test
46	Thermactor air not bypassed during self-test
51	-40°F indicated ECT sensor circuit open
52	PSPS circuit open
52	PSPS did not change states
53	TPS circuit above maximum voltage
54	-40°F indicated ACT, sensor circuit open
55	Key power circuit low
57	NPS circuit failed open
61	254°F indicated ECT, circuit grounded
63	TPS circuit below minimum voltage
64	254°F indicated ACT, circuit grounded
67	NPS circuit failed closed, A/C on during self-test
67	NDS circuit open, A/C on during self-test
72	Insufficient MAP change during dynamic response test
73	Insufficient TP change during dynamic response test
74	BOO switch circuit open
75	BOO switch circuit closed, ECA input open
77	Operator error (dynamic response/cylinder balance test)
78	Power interrupt detected
81	AM2 circuit failure (OCC test)
82	AM1 circuit failure (OCC test)

(Continues)

TYPICAL FORD DIAGNOSTIC TROUBLE CODES (Continued)

84	EVR circuit failure (OCC test)
85	CANP circuit failure (OCC test)
87	Fuel pump test failed (OCC test)
89	CCO circuit failure (OCC test)
91	EGO sensor input indicates system lean (cylinders 5-8)
92	EGO sensor input indicates system rich (cylinders 5-8)
94	Thermactor air system inoperative (cylinders 5-8, dual EGO)
98	Hard fault present, **FMEM MODE**
99	Idle not learned, ignore codes 12 and 13

TYPICAL CHRYSLER DIAGNOSTIC TROUBLE CODES

11	Distributor reference circuit		54	Distributor signal circuit
12	Battery feed to logic module recently lost		55	End of test sequence
13	MAP sensor circuit (vacuum)		88	Start of test sequence
14	MAP sensor circuit (electrical)			
15	Vehicle speed sensor			
16	Loss of battery voltage			
21	Oxygen sensor circuit			
22	Coolant temperature circuit			
23	Charge temperature circuit (turbo)			
24	Throttle position circuit			
25	Automatic idle speed circuit			
26	Fuel (peak injection current not reached)			
27	Fuel (no current in diagnostic transistor)			
31	Purge solenoid			
32	Powerloss lamp circuit			
33	A/C wide-open throttle circuit			
34	EGR solenoid circuit			
34	Spare driver circuit			
35	Fan relay circuit			
36	Spare driver circuit			
37	Shift indicator circuit (manual)			
41	Charging system			
42	Auto shutdown relay circuit			
43	Ignition and fuel control interface			
44	Logic module			
44	Battery temperature out of range			
45	Overboost (turbo)			
46	Battery voltage high			
47	Battery voltage low			
51	Oxygen feedback system			
51	Closed-loop latched lean			
52	Closed-loop latched rich			
52	Logic module			
53	Logic module			
53	ROM bit sum fault			

TYPICAL GENERIC OBD II POWERTRAIN DIAGNOSTIC TROUBLE CODES

PO102	MAF sensor circuit low input		PO300	Random misfire detected
PO103	MAF sensor circuit high input		PO301	Cylinder #1 misfire detected
PO112	IAT sensor circuit low input		PO302	Cylinder #2 misfire detected
PO113	IAT sensor circuit high input		PO303	Cylinder #3 misfire detected
PO117	ECT sensor circuit low input		PO304	Cylinder #4 misfire detected
PO118	ECT sensor circuit high input		PO305	Cylinder #5 misfire detected
PO122	TP sensor circuit low input		PO306	Cylinder #6 misfire detected
PO123	TP sensor circuit high input		PO307	Cylinder #7 misfire detected
PO125	Insufficient coolant temperature to enter closed-loop fuel control		PO308	Cylinder #8 misfire detected
PO132	Upstream heated oxygen sensor (HO2S 11) circuit high voltage (Bank #1)		PO320	Ignition engine speed input circuit malfunction
PO135	Heated oxygen sensor heater (HTR 11) circuit malfunction		PO340	Camshaft position (CMP) sensor circuit malfunction
PO138	Downstream heated oxygen sensor (HO2S 12) circuit high voltage (Bank #1)		PO402	EGR flow excess detected (valve open at idle)
PO140	Heated oxygen sensor (HO2S 12 circuit no activity detected (Bank #1)		PO420	Catalyst system efficiency below threshold (Bank #1)
PO141	Heated oxygen sensor heater (HTR 12) circuit malfunction		PO430	Catalyst system efficiency below threshold (Bank #2)
PO152	Upstream heated oxygen sensor (HO2S 21) circuit high voltage (Bank #2)		PO443	Evaporative emission control system canister purge control valve (CANP) circuit malfunction
PO155	Heated oxygen sensor heater (HTR circuit malfunction		PO500	Vehicle speed sensor (VSS) malfunction
PO158	Downstream heated oxygen sensor (HO2S 22) circuit high voltage (Bank #2)		PO505	IAC system malfunction
			PO605	Powertrain control module (PCM) read only memory (ROM) test error
PO160	Heated oxygen sensor (HO2S 22) circuit no activity detected (Bank #2)		PO703	Brake on/off switch input malfunction
PO161	Heated oxygen sensor heater (HTR circuit malfunction		PO707	Manual lever position (MLP) sensor circuit low input
PO171	System (adaptive fuel) too lean (Bank #1)		PO708	Manual lever position (MLP) sensor circuit high input
PO172	System (adaptive fuel) too rich (Bank #1)			
PO174	System (adaptive fuel) too lean (Bank #2)			
PO175	System (adaptive fuel) too rich (Bank #2)			

MOST COMMONLY USED WIRING COLOR STANDARDS

RED — Is for + 12 volts

ORANGE OR

ORANGE WITH BLACK — is for battery positive (+) or ignition positive (+).

BLACK — is for ground. Everything connected to the negative (-) battery terminal is black.

BROWN — turns something off.

BLUE — is used to power lights and for sensitive information, such as transmitting small electronic signals.

PURPLE — is used to make momentary connections, like to a starter motor.

YELLOW — is for signal-type information, like a door switch turning on an alarm.

GREEN — is for information associated with contact points, such as interrupting coil current and tachometer impulse pickup wires.

WHITE — is for a pulse, also common in ignition signal processing.

CARTER-YF, YFA 1BBL	CARTER-BBS 1BBL	CARTER-BBD

TAG NUMBER — STAMPED NUMBER

TAG NUMBER

NU

CARTER-AFB, AVS 4BBL	CARTER-TQ THERMOQUAD 4BBL	FORD-MOTORCRAFT 1100, 1101, 1250

TAG NUMBER

STAMPED NUMBER

STAMPED NUMBER

TAG NUMBER

FORD-MOTORCRAFT 2BBL 2100, 2150	FORD-MOTORCRAFT 2BBL VARIABLE VENTURI 2700, 7200	FORD-MOTORCRAFT 740

TAG NUMBER

STAMPED NUMBER

TAG NUMBER

FORD-MOTORCRAFT 4BBL 4300, 4350	HOLLEY-1904, 1908, 1BBL 1920, 1960	HOLLEY-1909

TAG NUMBER

STAMPED NUMBER (MAIN BODY)

STAMPED NUMBER

STAMPED NUMBER (SIDE OF BOWL)

ST NL (SIDE

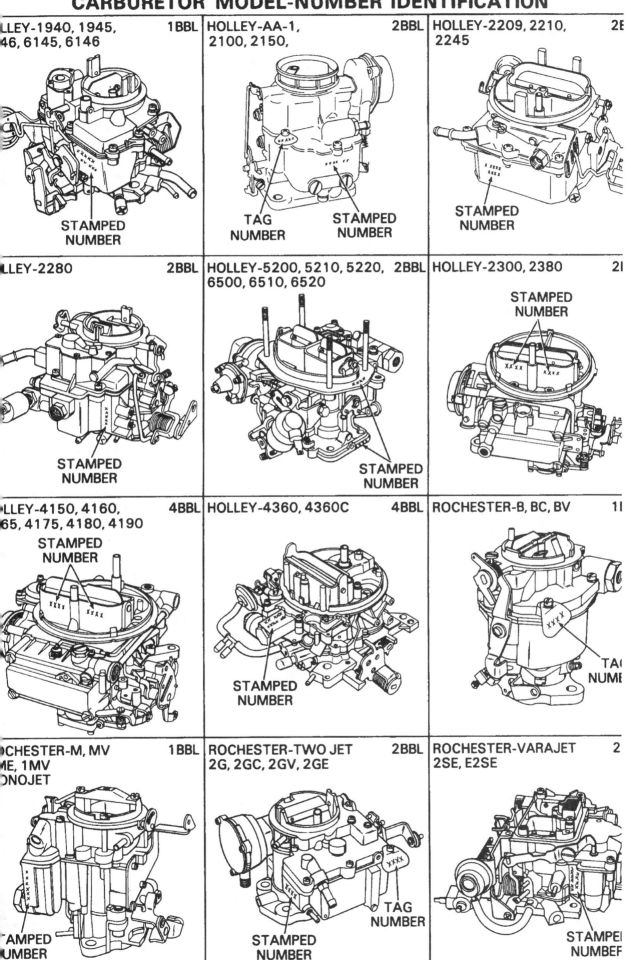

HOLLEY-1940, 1945, 46, 6145, 6146 — 1BBL
STAMPED NUMBER

HOLLEY-AA-1, 2100, 2150, — 2BBL
TAG NUMBER — STAMPED NUMBER

HOLLEY-2209, 2210, 2245 — 2B
STAMPED NUMBER

HOLLEY-2280 — 2BBL
STAMPED NUMBER

HOLLEY-5200, 5210, 5220, 6500, 6510, 6520 — 2BBL
STAMPED NUMBER

HOLLEY-2300, 2380 — 2B
STAMPED NUMBER

HOLLEY-4150, 4160, 65, 4175, 4180, 4190 — 4BBL
STAMPED NUMBER

HOLLEY-4360, 4360C — 4BBL
STAMPED NUMBER

ROCHESTER-B, BC, BV — 1B
TAG NUMBER

ROCHESTER-M, MV, ME, 1MV MONOJET — 1BBL
STAMPED NUMBER

ROCHESTER-TWO JET 2G, 2GC, 2GV, 2GE — 2BBL
TAG NUMBER — STAMPED NUMBER

ROCHESTER-VARAJET 2SE, E2SE — 2
STAMPED NUMBER

CARBURETOR MODEL-NUMBER IDENTIFICATION

ROCHESTER-DUALJET 210 2BBL M2MC, M2ME, E2ME, E2MC	ROCHESTER-4G, 4GC 4 BBL	ROCHESTER-QUADRAJET 2MC, 4M, 4MC, 4MV, M4MC, M4MV, E4MC, E4ME
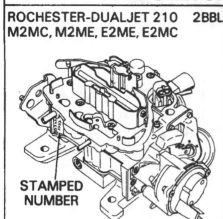 STAMPED NUMBER	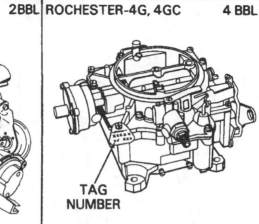 TAG NUMBER	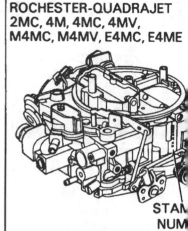 STAM NUM

THROTTLE BODY INJECTION MODEL - NUMBER IDENTIFICATION

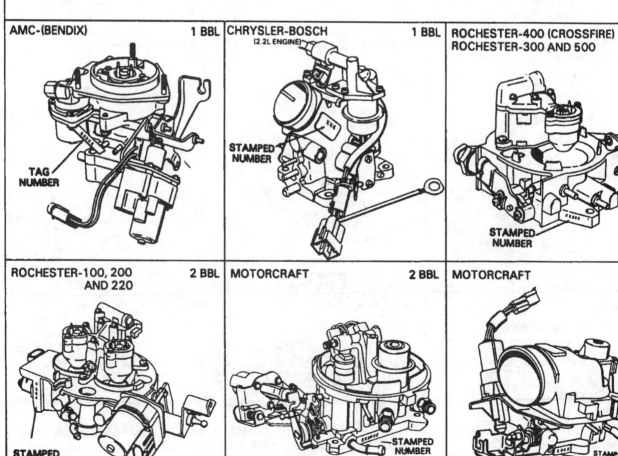

AMC-(BENDIX) 1 BBL	CHRYSLER-BOSCH 1 BBL (2.2L ENGINE)	ROCHESTER-400 (CROSSFIRE) ROCHESTER-300 AND 500
TAG NUMBER	STAMPED NUMBER	STAMPED NUMBER
ROCHESTER-100, 200 AND 220 2 BBL	MOTORCRAFT 2 BBL	MOTORCRAFT
STAMPED NUMBER	STAMPED NUMBER	STAMPED NUMBER

IMPORT CARBURETOR IDENTIFICATION

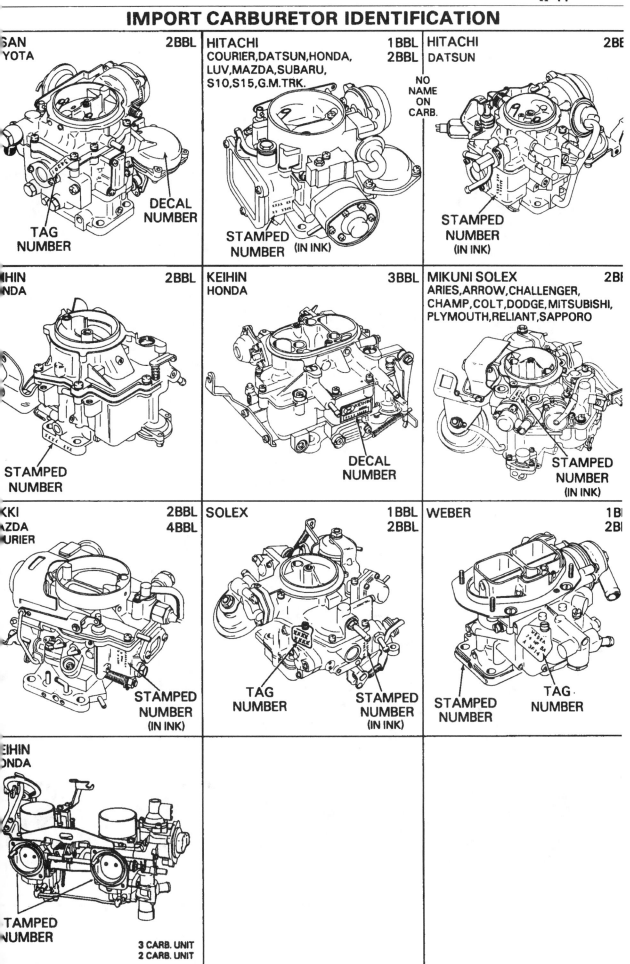

SAN 2BBL
YOTA

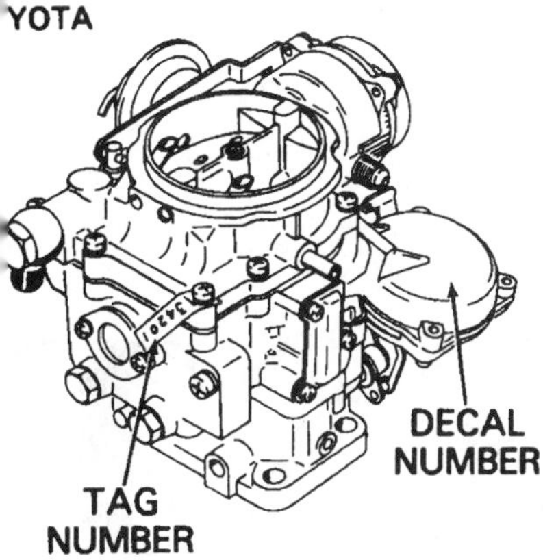
DECAL
NUMBER
TAG
NUMBER

HITACHI 1BBL 2BBL
COURIER,DATSUN,HONDA, LUV,MAZDA,SUBARU, S10,S15,G.M.TRK.

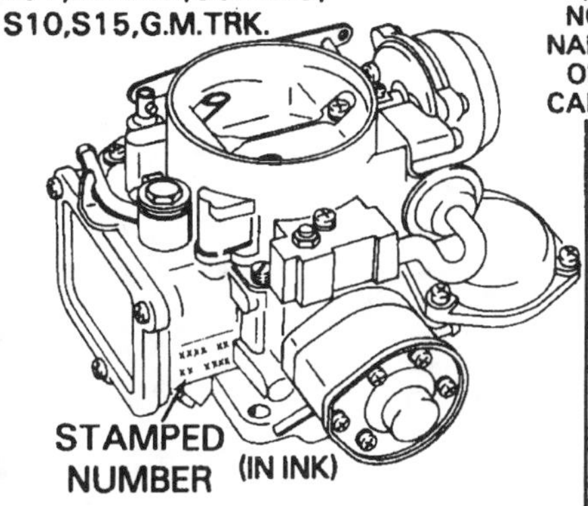
STAMPED
NUMBER (IN INK)

HITACHI 2BB
DATSUN

NO NAME ON CARB.

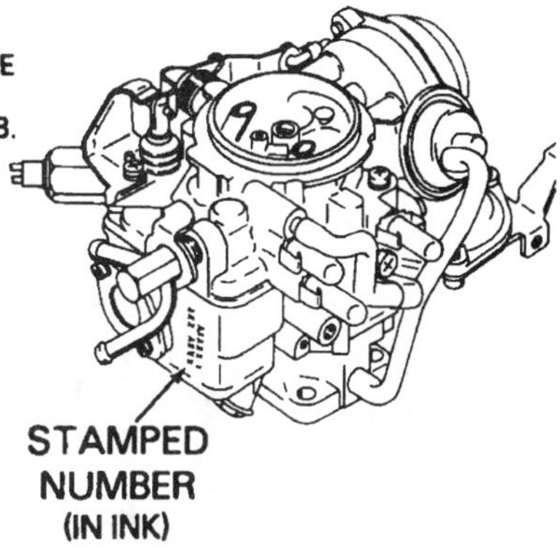
STAMPED
NUMBER
(IN INK)

HIN 2BBL
NDA

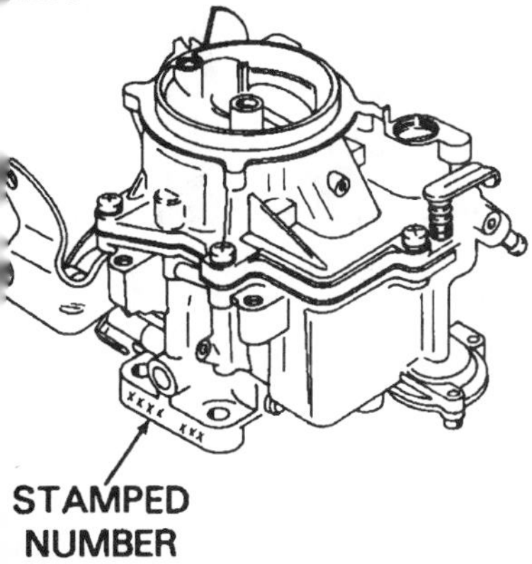
STAMPED
NUMBER

KEIHIN 3BBL
HONDA

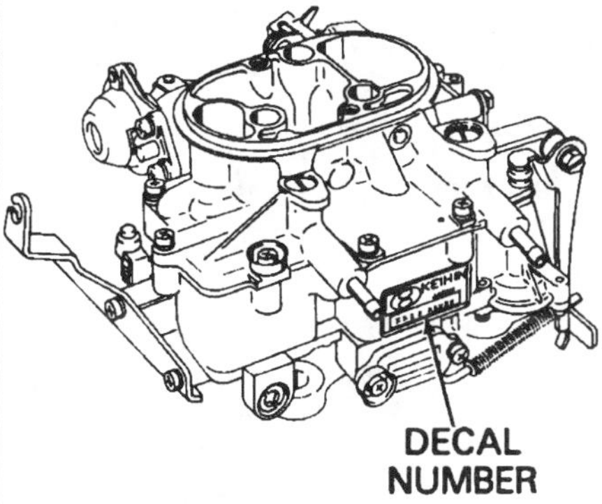
DECAL
NUMBER

MIKUNI SOLEX 2BB
ARIES,ARROW,CHALLENGER, CHAMP,COLT,DODGE,MITSUBISHI, PLYMOUTH,RELIANT,SAPPORO

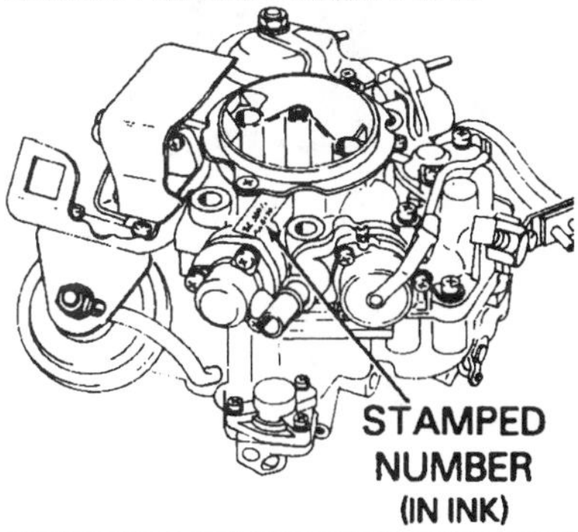
STAMPED
NUMBER
(IN INK)

KKI 2BBL 4BBL
ZDA
URIER

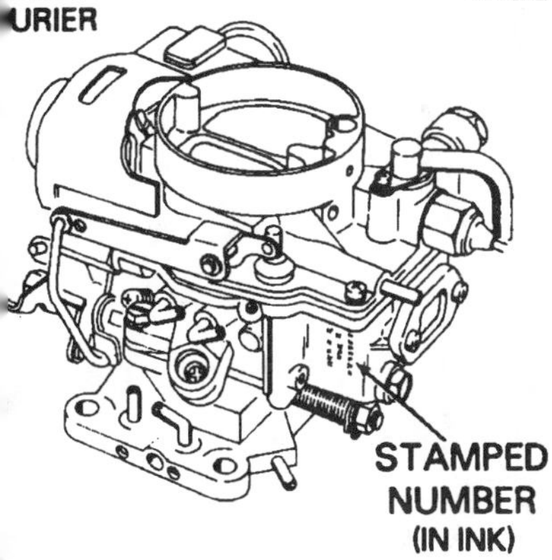
STAMPED
NUMBER
(IN INK)

SOLEX 1BBL 2BBL

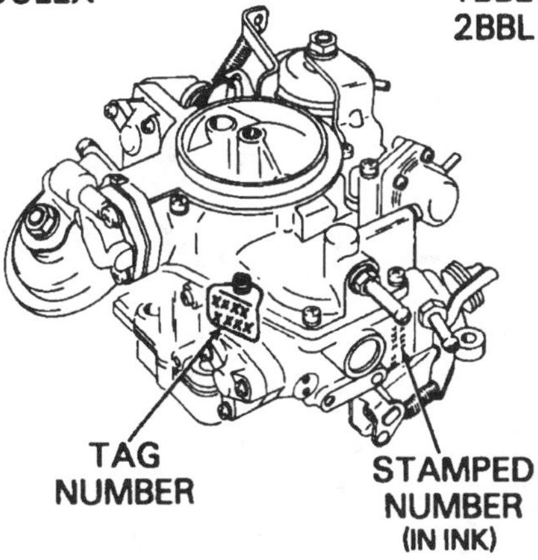
TAG
NUMBER
STAMPED
NUMBER
(IN INK)

WEBER 1BB 2BB

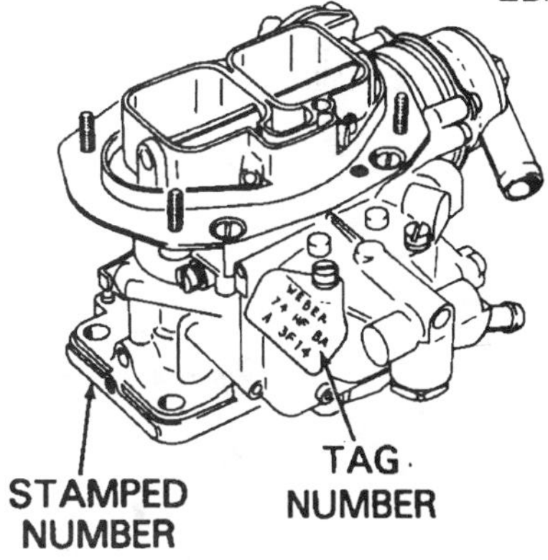
STAMPED
NUMBER
TAG
NUMBER

EIHIN
ONDA

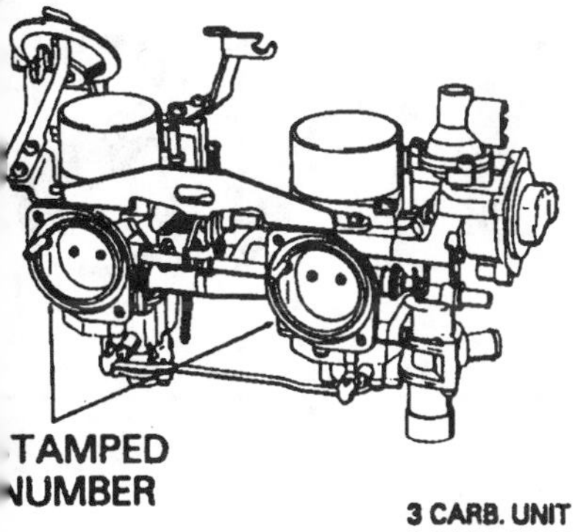
TAMPED
NUMBER

3 CARB. UNIT
2 CARB. UNIT

ONE TEST IS EQUAL TO 1,000 "EXPERT" OPINIONS

DIAGNOSTIC TOOL KIT

1. water spray bottle (small)
2. timing light
3. hand vacuum pump with vacuum gauge
4. compression gauge (screw-in type)
5. spark plug sockets/ratchet/extensions/universal joints
6. 5/32" I.D. vacuum hose (eight lengths each 2" long)
7. assortment of vacuum "T"s and plugs
8. 12-volt test light
9. spark plug gap gauge
10. long flexible magnet
11. terminal tools (picks) - OTC Tool No. 7733 (to remove terminals from connectors)
12. oil pressure sender socket - S & K Tool No. 4488
13. fuel pressure gauge (can be an old A/C gauge no longer used for A/C work)
14. oil pressure gauge (can be homemade from a brake hose and dash gauge) or oil pressure tester - Calvin Tool No. 836
15. noid light deluxe tester kit - OTC Tool No. 3050A
16. inspection mirror - Sears Craftsman Tool No. 94070
17. correction fluid ("White Out" or "Liquid Paper")
18. spark plug wire removal pliers or spark plug boot pliers - Calvin Tool No. 143
19. squeeze bottle for ATF (ketchup squeeze bottle OK)
20. tach tap #J-35812 or Ford & GM - OTC Tool No. 7152 or equivalent
21. spark tester ST-125 #J-26792 or KD-2756 or Thexton #404 adj. to 40 KV
22. 3" x 5" cards
*23. magnifying glass (lighted)
24. "T" pins in a film canister
25. anti-seize (Permatex #133A, small tube or #133K, 8 oz. can or 3M Brake Lube & Anti-Seize Compound Part #051135-08945, 9 oz. can)
26. acid brush (to apply anti-seize)
27. silicone grease or dielectric grease (Dow 111 or GE 661 preferred for spark plug wire boots or 3M Silicone Paste - Part #051135-08946, 8 oz.)
28. spark plug thread chaser - KD Tool No. 730
*29. infrared pyrometer
30. stethoscope - Sears Craftsman Tool No. 45164 or 3 feet of heater hose
*31. scan tool (Monitor 4000 or Snap-On preferred)
32. digital meter (Radio Shack 22-186, Fluke 87 or Kent-Moore J-39200 preferred)
33. logic probe (Radio Shack #22-303 or MCM Electronics)
34. oxygen sensor wrench or oxygen sensor socket - KD Tool No. 3259
35. Jumper wires with alligator clips (Radio Shack #278-1157)
36. flashlight
37. pocket screwdriver
38. clear RTV silicone
39. small file
40. exhaust back pressure tool made from an old O_2 sensor and tube
41. spray throttle plate cleaner with nozzle tube
42. small brass brush (to be used to clean throttle plates)
43. jumper wire for Fords - 1/4" male terminal at each end, 8"-10" long
44. pocket knife
45. two - 2 1/4" wide binder clips (for fender covers)
46. plastic tool box large enough for all of the above items

*Optional

TELEPHONE NUMBERS

Free Catalogs:

Crutchfield - car stereos, etc.	1-800-955-9009
Eastwood - automotive tools, supplies	1-800-345-1178
Kent-Moore - tool catalog	1-800-468-6657
Mouser Electronics	1-800-346-6873
MCM Electronics	1-800-543-4330

ASE Certification Test Study Guides:

GUIDE TO THE AUTOMOBILE CERTIFICATION EXAMINATION, 3rd Ed. Hughes, James G., Prentice-Hall, ISBN 0-13-365693-4	1-800-223-1360
CHEK-CHART STUDY GUIDES	1-800-662-6277
or outside USA	1-414-884-0908
MOTOR/AGE STUDY GUIDES	1-610-964-4240

"Nice to Know" Telephone Numbers:

ASE (Certification Test)	1-703-713-3800
Powergrip - rubber gloves	1-800-876-6866
Micro-flex - rubber gloves	1-415-872-3393
Helm Publishing Co. - service manuals	1-800-782-4356
Auto Safety Hotline	1-800-424-9393
Kent-Moore Tools	1-800-GM TOOLS
Packard - electrical components	1-800-722-5273
Fluke Meters	1-800-443-5853
General Motors (Main Number)	1-513-455-5000
SAE	1-412-776-4841
Bosch - technical booklets	1-800-937-2672
Faxon Literature - old factory manuals	1-800-458-2734
Prentice Hall Publishing Co	1-800-526-0485
GM S-10 Truck Plant Tours (Dayton, OH)	1-513-455-2776
Service Technicians Society (STS)	1-800-787-9596
Miller Special Tools (Chrysler tools)	1-313-522-6717
Hickok Electrical Instrument Co. (Ford tools)	1-216-541-8060
DIACOM (laptop computer program to retrieve scan data)	1-312-736-6633
Corvette Plant Tour Information	1-502-745-8000